Scriptwriting 2.0

WRITING FOR THE DIGITAL AGE

Marie Drennan

SAN FRANCISCO STATE UNIVERSITY

Yuri Baranovsky

HAPPY LITTLE GUILLOTINE FILMS

Vlad Baranovsky

HAPPY LITTLE GUILLOTINE FILMS

Holcomb Hathaway, Publishers • SCOTTSDALE, ARIZONA

Library of Congress Cataloging-in-Publication Data

Drennan, Marie.
  Scriptwriting 2.0 : writing for the digital age / Marie Drennan, San Francisco State University, Yuri Baranovsky, Happy Little Guillotine Films, Vlad Baranovsky, Happy Little Guillotine Films.
    pages cm
  Includes index.
  ISBN 978-1-934432-42-6 (print) — ISBN 978-1-934432-90-7 (ebook)
  1. Online authorship. 2. Motion picture authorship. I. Baranovsky, Yuri.
II. Baranovsky, Vlad. III. Title.
  PN171.O55D74 2013
  006.3—dc23

                                       2012039127

Screen Capture Actor Credits

p. 17: (top) Yuri Baranovsky, (middle) Drew Lanning, (bottom) Yuri Baranovsky, Rachel Risen; **p. 21:** (from left to right) Chad Yarish, Yuri Baranovsky, Skip Emerson; **p. 26:** Craig Bierko; **p. 33:** (facing us) Daniela DiIorio, Drew Lanning, (backs to us) Yuri Baranovsky, Wilson Cleveland; **p. 39:** Yuri Baranovsky, Rachel Risen; **p. 47:** (top, left to right) Wilson Cleveland, Drew Lanning, Daniela DiIorio, Yuri Baranovsky, (middle) Rachel Risen, (bottom) Daniela DiIorio, Drew Lanning; **p. 48:** Rachel Risen, Yuri Baranovsky; **p. 50:** Yuri Baranovsky, Rachel Risen; **p. 54:** Yuri Baranovsky, Mark Gantt; **p. 55:** Rachel Risen, Yuri Baranovsky; **p. 57:** (cowboy) Justin Morrison, (cowgirl) Alexis Boozer; **p. 82:** Drew Lanning, Alexis Boozer; **p. 83:** (left to right) Rachel Risen, Yuri Baranovsky, Alexis Boozer, Mark Gantt, Wilson Cleveland, Hillary Bergmann; **p. 84:** (left to right) Wilson Cleveland, Drew Lanning, Yuri Baranovsky, Alexis Boozer, Daniela DiIorio; **p. 91:** Yuri Baranovsky.

Holcomb Hathaway, Publishers, Inc.
8700 E. Via de Ventura Blvd., Suite 265
Scottsdale, Arizona 85258
480-991-7881
www.hh-pub.com

10 9 8 7 6 5 4 3 2 1

Print ISBN: 978-1-934432-42-6
Ebook ISBN: 978-1-934432-90-7

Printed in the United States of America.

Contents

Episode 2 and Beyond   *75*

Format   *87*

Copyright   *101*

Production   *113*

10 Reaching and Engaging Your Audience   *129*

Preface

People in media and mass communications are all about online and mobile content these days. They use it, they create it, and they want careers in it—which is great, because that's where the jobs are! And the fun part is that online and mobile entertainment is a reality that we're making up, together, as we go along. Today's media landscape offers creative opportunities unimagined by previous generations—and just as many challenges.

Scriptwriters and video producers and instructors in these areas have spent decades learning and teaching how to write structurally sound TV scripts, to direct a three-camera shoot from a control room, and to produce professional-quality news, sports, and magazine-format shows for local stations and cable access. But then YouTube, iMovie and the Flip camera appeared—and suddenly, everything changed. The shows got short (and weird). They abandoned genre and structure. They starting getting made fast and cheap, and looked it. So what is considered a "good" show in the age of user-generated content and DIY media? Did we mention that some shows are really weird?

But all is not lost. The "wild frontier" days of videoblogging and user-generated content—when nary a familiar genre or story structure was to be found—have become a bit more civilized. Online and mobile viewers are drifting away from the "lean forward" media culture of laboring to find good stuff to watch and assembling playlists just so they don't have to get up every four or five minutes to choose something to watch next. We're heading (or returning) to a "sit back" culture; we want it all to feel a little more like "real" TV. Luckily for scriptwriters and video producers, online shows now aim to deliver the same pleasures and gratifications as TV: engaging characters, show consistency across episodes, fairly regular new content that's easy to find (or that comes to us via subscriptions and feeds), and most importantly, stories that make sense. All of this depends on great writing.

Scriptwriting 2.0 is a book for those looking to explore online series while staying grounded in the essential skills and techniques of media writing. The authors—two award-winning web-series creators and a screenwriting instructor who took the leap from TV to online media—hope that this book will help readers explore their own scriptwriting paths with direction and success and inspire them to create engaging, entertaining online shows.

Acknowledgments

We would all like to thank the following reviewers, who offered constructive suggestions for improving this book. It is a better book because of their efforts. Thanks to Mark L. Arywitz, New York University; Glenda Cantrell-Williams, The University of Alabama; Jeanette Castillo, The Florida State University; Martie Cook, Emerson College; Kevin Corbett, Central Michigan University; Anthony R. Curtis, University of North Carolina at Pembroke; Daniel Cutrara, Arizona State University; Richard Endacott, University of Nebraska–Lincoln; Jeffrey N. Hirschberg, Buffalo State University; Robert D. Kalm, Quinnipiac University; Matthew Kaufhold, Drexel University; Joe Schuster, Webster University; Eric Sterbenk, Ithaca College; Nicholas Tanis, New York University; Richard Walter, University of California, Los Angeles; and Paige C. Waters, Ball State University.

From Marie Drennan: Many, many thanks to Rob Duncan, to my teachers and mentors Corless Smith and Phil Kipper, and to the intrepid student writers who inspired this book. Thanks also to my co-authors Vlad and Yuri Baranovsky for bringing their experience, wisdom and wit to my classroom; for giving so many students the opportunity to work with them; and especially for the great shows!

From Yuri Baranovsky: Thanks to Albert and Diana Baranovsky for the raising and the love and the just-about-everything. Thanks to Marie for finding us, telling us we're writing a book and then making the whole thing happen, and to Vlad for teaching me how to write and letting me steal his favorite toy car to give to that pretty girl in first grade. Thanks to Femke Groen for being my editing fairy and sprinkling the magic dust of proper English on my—I've lost track of the metaphor, but thank you for the endless support.

Thanks to Justin Morrison and Dashiell Reinhardt, the co-founders and co-producers of Happy Little Guillotine Films, without whom our shows wouldn't exist, our company wouldn't function, and my life would include a lot more shoe selling and a lot less art. Thanks to Daniela DiIorio, Hillary Bergmann, Dustin Toshiyuki, Drew Lanning, Hugo Martin and every other actor, crew member, and dearest friend who worked with us for what must be a billion hours, often for free, and who did it with unparalleled skill, love and humor.

Finally, thanks to our publisher for liking us, our editors (Gay Pauley and Lauren Salas) for making this book make sense, our *amazing* fans who have made every step of this possible and to you, the readers.

From Vlad Baranovsky: Thanks to Albert and Diana Baranovsky for filling my head with stories. To Monica and Maya Baranovsky for being the most supportive, patient, and loving family anyone can ask for. To Yuri Baranovsky for always being the voice in my head that says "but you can make this better, right?" Thanks to Marie Drennan for conceiving this book, to Dashiell Reinhardt and Justin Morrison for all things HLG, and to all of the amazing actors and crew who've made our shows happen.

Thanks to Lauren Salas and Gay Pauley at Holcomb Hathaway for their wisdom and guidance in putting together this book. And finally, thank you to all of our fans, without whose support and enthusiasm we would have never gotten into the web series racket in the first place.

INTRODUCTION
Writing for
Online Series

These are exciting times for writers. Not long ago, if you wanted to create entertainment content you had to move to Burbank and hope your spec scripts might get read by someone who knew someone who could get you a trial run on the writing staff of an obscure sitcom. But in the digital, online age, everyone can be a creator (and distributor) of their own creative works, such as the web series we discuss at length in this book.

Online episodic content has evolved along with the Internet. As the availability of bandwidth increased, it became possible to upload longer and higher quality video. Vlogging (videoblogging) boomed in 2006 when Jay Dedman formed the Yahoo! Videobloggers Group and organized Vloggercon. "Media democracy," or replacing a corporate-controlled, ratings-dependent mass media with creative work arising from real people, was all the rage. The dominant ethos among creators was to reject, subvert, and generally "talk back" to corporate media, especially TV. Ever since, as video sharing sites have proliferated, online content created by regular folks has become ubiquitous and infinite in its variety.

Writers of online series must undertake a range of creative decision-making that TV writers rarely need to worry about. Back in the day, a network sitcom needed 11 million viewers watching their TVs at a specific time to stay on the air. Online shows don't need 11 million viewers—or one million, or any minimum number—to air their work online. This frees web series creators to choose where they want to be on the "like TV—unlike TV" continuum. Traditional TV genres are familiar to audiences, so online shows that are straightforward sitcoms, dramas or dramedies are likely to draw in audiences that watch TV but are starting to get comfortable with shorter formats and online viewing. Many online creators stick with familiar genres but go rogue with premise, characters, setting, visual style, etc. Such content might draw a smaller audience, but that can actually be a good thing: Tapping in to a niche can generate a more dedicated, engaged community of viewers (see Chapter 10, Reaching and Engaging Your Audience).

The online age has also seen the demise of the "one person, one job" model (you're a writer *or* a director *or* an actor, etc.). These days, the writer is often the show creator and might also serve as editor, score composer, location scout, casting director, production manager and actor. With fewer people involved in writing and production, online shows can have a richer sense of an "auteur" than TV shows that have large writing staffs delivering scripts to the production team and the actors, all of whom then influence the overall story and aesthetics. In online series, creators can avoid having "too many cooks spoiling the soup" and maintain greater creative control. As a result, the online video landscape teems with content that reflects the individuality of the creators.

The potential downside to all of this is what writers call "the tyranny of the blank page," that terrible moment (or hour, or week) when you sit down to write and realize that blinking cursor isn't going to move until you decide what you're doing. This is a natural part of the creative process. Even if you have a pretty clear idea of what you'd like to create, you still have a lot to think through. You won't realize how much until you get further into the process. This book will help you clarify on a deep level what you're trying to do. The goals are to confront all that is vague and undefined in your idea, premise, and script; polish everything that is less than crystal clear; and banish everything that is not downright muscular in its service to your story.

GETTING STARTED

Before you start to write, consider the purpose of your show, and based on that, *what will work*. Here are three practical questions to help you generate—and narrow down—an initial list of possible show concepts.

1. *Where will the show "live"?* It might live independently as a standalone product available on YouTube and other host sites, or its own dedicated website; in this case, the show's purpose is simply to attract and entertain viewers. Or the show might be a series of episodes or installments that live as segments within a longer magazine-format, variety or news show. It might be designed to live on a curated channel or be included in playlists featuring topical or genre-specific content. These factors will affect the choices you make regarding your show's structure, thematic unity and desired audience.

2. *How long will the show run (how many episodes or installments)?* Is the goal to deliver a certain number of scripts for production (for example, in collaboration with a production class)? Is it to begin a project that will continue beyond the duration of your scriptwriting class? Do you have enough material for a show that goes on for many seasons, or is your project more like a miniseries? These factors will help determine the scope and nature of your show's premise. They will also be partly determined by your production resources and plans.

3. *To what degree, and in what ways, must the show be episodic?*
   The installments might be parts of an ongoing narrative,
   broken where necessary into acts that fit the desired/allotted
   airtime (like TV soap operas, novel adaptations and other kinds
   of miniseries). Or they might follow sitcom or crime drama
   structure, each episode developing and resolving a self-contained
   situation, while overarching storylines and relationships evolve
   across episodes and even seasons. Or the episodes might be of a
   more standalone nature, connected only topically, thematically
   or by using a regular cast.

DESIGN CONCEPT AND PRODUCTION PARAMETERS

Whether or not production is a required part of your scriptwriting course or part of your own plan as a creator, one of your tasks as a creator of online content is to design your show so that it can survive and thrive on the Internet. A web show is different from a TV show or a short film for many reasons: the mechanisms of distribution and audience reception, the rapidly emerging and evolving styles of online entertainment, and the broad range of ways to define and quantify success (massive numbers of views; cult status within a smaller, select population; commercial sponsorship and profit, etc.).

From the get-go, you'll want to consider the aesthetic of your show. Ask yourself two questions: "What is it possible to do with the equipment, locations and cast available to me?" and "What aesthetic best serves my show's content and 'job description'?" It isn't always necessary (or wise) to aim for high-end production quality; online, the "DIY" style can be more appropriate and appealing. What matters is that the design concept, production aesthetic and writing style are compatible and consistent. This will depend on three key factors:

1. *Equipment.* This includes cameras, lights, microphones and
   beyond. What can you get your hands on, either through your
   class/department or your own resources? Many of today's smartphones are perfectly serviceable, but it's possible that your show

requires a more polished appearance. (Sound quality is non-negotiable. Don't skimp on that, ever.)

2. *Locations.* Where will you shoot your scenes? This isn't just a matter of finding a restaurant, warehouse or library that will give you permission; it's also largely determined by the portability of your cast, crew and equipment, and by light and sound factors (unblockable windows or skylights; ambient noise). Shooting on a stage set or in a few familiar locations can enhance the show's continuity and sense of being a "real show"; on the other hand, part of the fun of online series is *not* doing things the way they're usually done for TV. The question is what best serves your show's aesthetic.

3. *Cast.* Many online show creators use amateur actors, often including the show's writers and crew (plus their friends and family). It is possible to design and write a show that doesn't require impeccable acting—though viewers have come to expect online content to transcend the "goofy, low-budget" style that was prevalent only a few years ago. Consider collaborating with students in theater, cinema, music, dance and communication departments, as well as community theater and improv troupes.

Throughout the scriptwriting section of this book, you will be encouraged to think about your show *as a web series*—which means keeping production design, copyright, distribution and community-building in mind. These topics are covered in detail in Chapter 10, Reaching and Engaging Your Audience, which (if you are serious about producing your show) you should read and refer to as you write your scripts.

Now, let the ride begin!

ABOUT THE AUTHORS

Before we jump in, we'd like you to know more about who, exactly, is writing this, what experience we have, and why we've chosen the shows we discuss in this book.

Vlad and Yuri Baranovsky have been writing for web series since before writing for new media was a thing. The brothers created *Break a Leg* while Vlad was still a creative writing student and Yuri was newly out of community college, where he tentatively studied drama. They begged, borrowed and sometimes politely stole and then returned cameras, lights, locations and just about everything else to make the show possible. The cast and crew worked for free, and for over three years, Vlad and Yuri shot *Break a Leg* between full-time jobs, school, relationships and life. As *Break a Leg* gained popularity online, the brothers, along with two business partners, created Happy Little Guillotine Films (www.hlgfilms.com), a production company focused specifically on creating online content. With HLG Films, Vlad and Yuri created multiple large-scale branded campaigns and series. One recent project, *Leap Year,* has now completed its second season, which attracted millions of viewers and write-ups from many major publications.

Marie Drennan has been teaching scriptwriting since before the dawn of the Internet, and she likes it better now. One reason for that: unlike in days past when scripts were graded and handed back and usually forgotten, now students can get their work up on the screen for all the world to see. They can graduate with a finished episode or even a whole series to show prospective sponsors, investors, employers and cast and crew. Another reason that teaching scriptwriting for online series is more exciting now is the greater creative freedom enjoyed by creators. Today's online series writers are less bound by conventions regarding subject matter, story pacing, realism (or surrealism)—so much is open to the writer's imagination. At the same time, crafting episodes that tell a story and feel "finished" in a limited number of minutes is a hard job. Just as there are techniques and conventions for structuring traditional TV sitcoms and dramas, there are strategies for presenting unconventional work in a way that surprises but doesn't lose the audience.

The shows discussed in this book include *Break a Leg* and *Leap Year,* both created, written and produced by Vlad and Yuri Baranovsky, and *Coach* and *The Defenders of Stan,* both of which enjoyed long runs on Channel 101, a monthly competition to which anyone can submit a pilot episode (nudge, nudge). This book includes detailed accounts of the writing and production of *Break a Leg* and *Leap Year,* as well as a sample script and a crash-course in online publicity and distribution, by those who made it happen. *Coach* and *The Defenders of Stan* were chosen because they are both set in "abnormal" worlds presented as normal (a challenge many web series writers take on); they develop characters' deep feelings and motivations (even though the shows are playful in concept); and they illustrate key dramatic principles with tremendous economy (possibly the hardest part of all).

Our goal for this book is to offer you practical, real-world tools to begin creating for online content, coupled with the inspiration to do it! We hope you discover both in the following pages.

ACCESSING THE WEB SERIES WE TALK ABOUT

We have provided two ways for you to view the several web series we discuss throughout the book. First, we include a general URL for the series website, if one is available. For example, here are the addresses for the two web series created by Yuri and Vlad Baranovsky, which we discuss most often in the book:

Leap Year, www.leapyear.tv

Break a Leg, www. breakaleg.tv

On these sites you will be able to access all seasons and all episodes of the series.

Next, when we discuss specific episodes of these two series, we provide specific URLs that will take you directly to the episode. We have gathered these episodes on Vimeo so that they are easily accessible and ad-free, and to help prevent you from encountering broken links.

For the other series not created by the book's co-authors, the episodes will be linked through sites such as YouTube and Channel 101, which means we're less able to control whether the links are intact. If you encounter broken links, please feel free to email feedback@ hh-pub.com with that information (or any feedback you may have about the book). Thank you.

Enjoy watching!

C H A P T E R **2**

What's Your Show About?

THE IDEA PHASE

You've probably got lots of ideas for shows. Some of them sound like instant hits; some seem like they could attract a cult following; some could be totally loony. On network or cable TV, only the first (and rarely the second) category would be considered for development. But web writing isn't about copying what's on TV. So which of your ideas should you pick to actually write and produce? What's a "good idea" in online series?

The answer is that every idea *might* be a good one. It's not a question of how weird it is or isn't. In the idea-generating phase, you don't have to rule anything out. If an idea grabs you, let yourself run with it. Just for a while, mute the nagging voice that keeps saying, "That's too weird, no one will want to watch that," or "That's too much like a show that's already on."

If you anticipate production problems, you'll find a way around them. This is the creative stage that author Stephen King calls "writing with the door closed." You get to do anything you want, without suffering consequences or criticism.

Generating Ideas

An idea can come from anywhere. It could be a "what-if" scenario: What if everyone in the world got superpowers? What if a college accepted an international student who was raised by wolves? Or the idea could be primarily a setting and/or group of characters: young tech whizzes working "from home" in an Internet café; international spies undercover at a mall food court; retired astronauts competing in a chili cook-off. And yes, you can even have a show about regular people living regular lives and having regular problems (though we'll talk in a moment about whether it can be *too* familiar). Let every idea be a "good one." At this point you're generating, rather than critiquing or editing.

Going Beyond Listing Scenarios

Stick with the idea for a bit, just for the sake of exploring how you might turn it into a show. Who would the main character be, and what supporting characters would you need? Imagine you got a contract to write five episodes; what kinds of things would happen in each installment? Don't tell yourself it won't work. Instead, force yourself to determine how you would make it work. What you're trying to do is practice turning an idea into a framework for a series of stories—in other words, a *show premise*.

Crafting a Premise

Now the work gets a little bit harder. Audiences don't watch ideas; they watch shows. More specifically, they watch stories. A show premise is an idea that has been shaped and refined to support an ongoing series of stories. The premise answers the question: "Who and what is your show about?" It is the basic framework of the show, the overarching "reality" that remains constant in every episode. It consists of clearly defined characters interacting in an environment that generates a steady stream of drama and conflict (even in comedies). Small details might change over time: relationships begin and end, secondary characters come and go, etc. But the elements that generate the drama—these central characters, in these basic circumstances—remain constant. The premise provides a foundation upon which the writer builds individual episodes.

Often, a writer will get an idea for a show about his or her friends, coworkers, family, etc. It makes sense: Write what you know, right? We all know people who are so inherently interesting, weird or funny that they could easily be the subject of a show. Now add a location: say you're going to write a show about the crazy but fabulous people you worked with at the tourist resort last summer. It's a fine idea, but notice that at this stage, you still don't have a *premise*. All you have is an idea for some characters and a place to put them. Tons of zany stuff might happen, but there's no real framework to connect the episodes other than the fact that the audience will see the same actors and the same set each time.

This is why aspiring writers are often advised to *never write a show about your friends*. That sounds crazy at first. Obviously, there are many shows about friends; there was even an extremely successful TV sitcom called *Friends*. There are probably more shows about friends than there are about families. But this advice has nothing to do with objecting to shows about groups of friends. It's a warning to writers against making a hard task even harder: that of mistaking an idea (in this case, an idea about characters) for a premise.

A show without a clear premise, even if it's crammed with great acting and great jokes, feels aimless, like a highlight reel. To viewers, your friends (or coworkers, or family members) might be delightful characters with many amusing quirks, but without a *story framework* in which the comedy operates, the jokes are simply gags that don't add up to anything.

So how do you get from idea to premise? Let's look at the web series *The Defenders of Stan*, which started with the idea of a world where everyone is a superhero. That's an irresistible idea—but it

Why you should not focus on your friends

Think about it for a moment, and be honest. If you didn't know your friends, would you really watch a show that featured them doing what they do—being themselves? Of course your friends are interesting to you, because you know them, have shared experiences with them and can put their words and actions in a context that gives them meaning. Even if your video captured their most hilarious ten minutes ever, or if you were to edit and string together a series of their funniest moments, would people who didn't know them watch for more than a couple of minutes? How often would an audience want to see a new episode? Probably one would be more than enough.

isn't quite a premise yet. It could be interpreted a million different ways. Is it going to be an action-adventure series, showcasing different heroes? Is it going to be a comedy about heroes with silly powers? Is it going to focus on a love relationship, a vendetta, a threat against humanity? *Who* and *what* are we actually going to see when we watch the show?

The idea needs to be narrowed into a specific dramatic direction. Here's one way to give it focus: "There's only one guy, Stan, left on

http://ny.channel101.com/view.php?epid=176

earth without superpowers." Now we have a premise. We also have one character (Stan) we can get to know. The context of the show will be that everyone on earth has superpowers, but the show will be *about* Stan. Each episode will tell a story in which Stan faces the situation of being the last "normal" person on earth. This focus will be extremely helpful when it comes time to craft individual episodes, because it gives you, the writer, a solid framework for your stories. You might still incorporate superhero showcases, love interests, silly powers and a threat against humanity—but now you have the glue to make it a coherent series instead of a loose collection of characters and events. Everything that happens in your show will point back to the premise that there's only one guy left who doesn't have superpowers.

Think again about writing five or ten or twenty episodes of your series. This is the point where you want to really test your idea to see if it can be developed into an ongoing stream of stories. Ideas tend to "want" to be expressed in a certain structure or medium. Some want to be feature-length films; some want to be hour-long TV dramas or half-hour sitcoms; some want to be comedy sketches or stand-up monologues. Is your idea suited for the short online series format? Could you get at least five episodes out of your idea, or is it more of a one-time, standalone kind of thing? It can be hard to set a good idea aside, but it's better to do it before you get stuck trying to write a series that doesn't want to be one.

Luckily, there's one more thing you can use to make your idea into a show. In addition to the premise, you need to find your show's central question. This is the *throughline* that gives your show coherence: It's the point of the show.

The Central Question

You've started with an idea and crafted it into a premise. Now ask: why should the audience care? Even if your show is a light-hearted comedy, or a darkly ironic one, and "caring" doesn't sound like what you want the audience to do, your real goal is to sustain interest—which means the audience must care enough about someone or something to find out what happens next. Viewers might describe the experience as liking, enjoying, being curious about, being amused by, instead of "caring"—but none of these can happen without some meaning arising from the action and dialogue. Even if we laugh cruelly at a character's foolishness or suffering, we care enough to understand his or her predicament and respond with genuine interest.

Take Stan, for instance. Why do we care about Stan? He must in some way attract us and arouse our empathy. He must be like you and me. How would you feel if you were the last person on earth without superpowers? What would you do? What would you hope to gain? What would you risk to get it?

It might seem odd to treat an impossible, fictional scenario "realistically," but stories have to contain something the audience can relate to, even if it's in a comedic context. What is Stan's daily life like? What does he think about? Does he have any friends? What does he do all day while everyone else is flying around fighting crime? Probably, he's going to be very lonely. Maybe he'll be ignored or patronized. He will almost certainly suffer, which will help the audience empathize with him. You can see how we're starting to build up some emotional interest.

But no one will want to watch this character sitting around, moping about his condition. We need to see him take action, to *struggle*. He's got to somehow fix his situation. We know he's one of the few remaining people without superpowers—but what does he want or need, and how will he strive for it in each episode? How can we round out our premise? What are we waiting and watching to find out about him?

Stan is struggling to find happiness—the same thing everyone struggles for in life—but under extraordinary circumstances. His specific struggle is to find happiness *in a world that has left him behind*. Now we have a central question: *Will Stan find a way out of his lonely isolation?* In each episode, we'll watch him struggle with a specific challenge that relates to his quest, and we will feel his suffering as well as his hope. Although the show's *premise* is intended to be fantastic and outside the bounds of human experience, the *central question* brings it back to a feeling everyone can relate to: not wanting to be left out.

Here is the premise of the web series *Coach* (www.channel101. com/episode/953): The world's best coach is so motivating and exciting that it causes fatal brain aneurisms in his athletes. Like all premises, this could play out in a number of ways. The coach could use his power to kill rival teams; he could become an aneurism-for-hire hitman; he could train a younger version of himself, hoping to share his talents with the world (without murdering anyone). None of these premises is inherently better than the others. Any or all of them could work as long as the show has a strong, clear central question. In the pilot episode, we see Coach giving an impassioned pre-game pep talk to a girls' basketball team. The girls drop dead. The opening credit sequence shows Coach one year later, a lonely drifter. Walking along the highway shoulder, hunted and on the run, he spots an empty car and tries to steal it. The owner, a hapless and amiable teenaged boy, appears and thanks Coach for helping start the car. The boy gives Coach a ride into town but it soon becomes clear the boy urgently needs coaching on his driving skills. Coach finds his motivating power is strong enough to save them both from a terrible crash. The boy is so grateful and eager to learn to drive that Coach, realizing there is hope of returning to his former life (and unable to suppress his natural motivating instincts), stays and teaches the boy. At the end of the episode, Coach's big speech gives the boy an aneurism and kills him. Again, Coach is on the run, desperate to avoid harming others but also tormented by his irrepressible instincts to motivate. In his own personal hell, he is doomed to a life of hiding, guilt and shame. (Sounds hilarious, right? This kind of dark comedy has strong appeal for some viewers, but not all.)

The series' premise, which is rather silly on the surface, gains emotional dimension from its focus on the main character's inner struggle. The show captures the painful irony of possessing a tremendous power to help, but being unable to use it without inflicting terrible harm. The show's external situations and crises are anchored in the context of Coach's deep suffering. We see his hopeful attempt to regain his identity and reclaim his life, and we understand his agony when his efforts end in tragedy. But it isn't just his career that he wants back. He wants redemption. This man is desperate, running from the law, humanity and himself. This creates a strong central question: *Will Coach find a way out of his personal hell?* The depth of the question is juxtaposed with the show's goofy characters and situations and gives viewers a reason to care and to want to see more episodes.

Not all online shows have a premise as high-concept as *The Defenders of Stan* or *Coach*. Let's look at the path from idea to premise to central question for a show about regular people. Start with the idea of a person having to choose between keeping his secure but boring job and risking everything for a better career. That's an idea that a lot of people will relate to; everyone has fantasized about it at some point. We don't quite have a premise, though. Who and what will this show really be about?

The idea needs details: a main character, supporting and opposing characters, and a setting or set of circumstances in which they struggle for happiness. Most importantly, we need more information about the guy, so that he becomes a character we can be curious and concerned about.

In the first season of *Leap Year* (www.leapyear.tv) Aaron is a hardworking and honest man who passionately loves his wife; he is also deeply insecure about deserving her and afraid of failing to take care of her—and she's five months pregnant. Everyone at his company is pretty sure they're about to get laid off, so he's already in danger. He is also about to turn 30, so he is vulnerable to the existential self-questioning that comes with major life milestones. His friends want to strike out on their own and start their own companies, and Aaron is pressured to take the leap as well. All of this terrifies him. He feels himself to be on the brink both of great happiness and of total ruin.

Now we have a premise: A man takes on a risky new career and struggles on the brink of great happiness and total ruin. An idea that began as universal has been narrowed down to one main character whom we can engage with, in a specific set of circumstances that will challenge him in every episode.

Notice that *Leap Year,* Season 1, is really about two different things. The first is the success or failure of Aaron's new career, which is an external question. The audience can relate to the risk being taken, and can feel invested in Aaron's triumphs and defeats.

The second question is Aaron's psychological and emotional survival—the internal question. The first time we meet Aaron, he is worrying. He's worrying about losing his job, not being able to support the baby that's on its way and letting Lisa down. But his worrying goes even deeper. Aaron, we perceive, is a chronically, maybe even neurotically, worried person. He's scared. All the time. Notice how the writers have designed Aaron as an ideal character to place in the following specific dilemma.

https://vimeo.com/47871716

Near the end of the pilot episode (Episode 1) of *Leap Year,* a character makes this speech: "Life happens. The job you have today might not be the job you have tomorrow. The life you have today is probably not the same life you're going to be living next week. Embracing the little moments, taking risks, making leaps—these are what this whole thing is all about."

This articulates the underlying theme of the show: It takes a lot of courage to live life fully. This theme is expressed as Aaron's personal struggle in the last scene, in which he asks his wife to tell him every-

thing is going to be okay, and he repeats the word "okay." We can see that Aaron wants to believe in him-self and in new possibilities, but he struggles with basic fear. Everything that happens to Aaron and every-thing he does will be underscored by this theme of having to overcome fear and believe in the great life he has. So the internal central question of the show is: *Will Aaron succeed in overcoming his fear and opening himself to life's worthwhile risks?*

As we get to know Aaron and the surrounding characters bet-ter, we will grow to understand how life's challenges affect him personally, so that even though we're watching "regular" people with "regular" problems, it feels as though what we're seeing is special and unique. We respond to the emotional core of the show. And we feel that way because we've been drawn in to the show's central question. The question won't be answered in one episode; it is the emotional and psychological throughline that will give the series its depth as each episode unfolds.

DESIGNING YOUR CHARACTERS

*I*magine your friends are talking about something that someone did. What's the absolute first thing you want to know? *Who* it was, of course. Otherwise you have no context, no way to know how to feel. If your friends keep talking without telling you who did it or who it happened to, you'll feel a growing sense of urgency to know.

That *urgency to know* is what you want your audience to feel. You want to get them engaged and curious right away, from the very first minute of your story, so the first thing you do is give them a "who." Later you'll put that character in a "did something/had something happen" situation, and you'll have a story. But what the audience needs most is someone to focus on and get to know.

You began developing your main character, and probably some supporting characters, when you were figuring out your show's central question. In further designing your characters, you aren't just creating interesting people; you're creating the source(s) of your show's drama and conflict. Your characters give your show its emotional depth (whether that's a little or a lot) and its point. In other words, each character is there to fulfill a dramatic function. Your task is to "hire" the best people for that job.

The Main Character

Ask yourself two questions about your main character. One is: "Who is this person?" The other is: "What is he or she struggling for?"

Sitcom characters have personalities that are tightly defined by a few obvious traits that are usually exaggerated and sometimes absurd. In *The Office,* Dwight Schrute is always grimly focused on survival tactics; Jim Halpert is the "normal guy" who maintains his sanity by pranking, teasing and generally tormenting Dwight. In *The Big Bang Theory,* Sheldon Cooper is sarcastic, logical and more than a little socially awkward; Penny consistently contrasts him by being scatterbrained and outgoing. As the series progresses, the characters might get fleshed out a little; we might learn more about the characters' histories, and we might see them grow a little or learn from their mistakes. But it's a guarantee that at the end of every episode, each character's defining traits are completely intact and unchanged, and will be just as obvious at the beginning of the next episode.

Even if your show is not a sitcom, you will find that well-defined characters clarify and strengthen your story. They don't need to be exaggerated or clownish, but the audience should be able to discern enough about them to understand their drive to overcome each crisis. And this understanding needs to happen immediately; as soon as the story opens, the character should be revealed and reinforced through dialogue and action. Although some TV dramas open with a "Last time on . . ." summary, these focus on plot; they are not used to establish or explain characters' basic personalities. *Dr. Horrible's Singalong Blog* is a good example. The pilot episode (http://www.youtube.com/watch?v=apEZpYnN_1g) opens with Dr. Horrible practicing his evil laugh, trying different styles and seeming awkward and uncomfortable; he mentions that he's working with a vocal coach. As he talks about his hopes of joining the Evil League of Evil, he reveals his basically friendly nature and a good deal of insecurity. Already we know that this is not a really bad guy.

Another good example is *Roommates* (www.channel101.com/episode/879). The premise is that Tom and Harry share an apartment with Google. In the show, Google is not just a human manifestation of the company's essence; he *is* Google. As Google "helpfully" learns about Tom and Harry by photographing every inch of their apartment (including personal files) and recommending restaurants and purchases based on their previous online search histories, Harry appreciates the help while Tom is annoyed by the invasion of his privacy and suspicious of Google's motives. From the beginning of the pilot episode, we understand that Harry is the part of us that relies on and is glad to have Google, and Tom is the part of us that can't help but be a little creeped out by Google's limitless reach into our lives.

However, even if you want your character to seem real and complex, remember that the audience can't get to know everything about a person in 30 or 60 minutes, let alone five or ten. You only have enough time to show a few basic traits, whether they are exaggerated and clownish or subtle and realistic.

The real magic of such tightly defined or exaggerated characters is that they have a limited range of responses to the world around them. Unlike real people, they can't choose to think or behave one way in this situation and a different way in the next; they behave as they've been defined, consistently, no matter what is going on. Whatever the style and tone of your show, clearly defining your characters will allow you to use them in each episode without having to re-introduce them. It gives the audience a "who" right away, no explanation needed, so the story can start immediately. Crafting characters is not just a matter of making them interesting or funny; it's also for the sake of clarity and efficiency in the script.

The importance of suffering

Now for the second question about your main character: What is he or she struggling for? Remember that you aren't writing a character study; you're writing a *story*. The question "Who is this person?" doesn't get interesting until we see him or her moving through the world, interacting with people, facing conflict and solving problems. Yet, at the same time, the audience needs to know who the character is so that they can appreciate the significance of those conflicts and problems. A story is stuff that happens to someone, but the stuff doesn't grab us unless we understand that someone.

If the audience has a clear understanding of who your character is, they will understand what makes him or her suffer. Your job as a writer, as horrible as it sounds, is to make us care about a character and then make that character's life really hard. In fact, fiction as a whole—in novels, films, plays, and TV shows—is designed to create turmoil, emotional pain, and problem after problem for a character. Thus, we need to know the character well enough to appreciate why a particular situation is especially difficult for him or her, and to feel invested in his or her struggle. The situations you create would probably be challenging for anyone, but your character is designed to suffer from that situation more than the average person would.

In *Break a Leg* (www.breakaleg.tv/), David Penn is ill-equipped for the situation he finds himself in. He's a struggling writer who's a bit bewildered and out of his league, feeling grateful just to be working at all; he's not very confident, which makes him go along with a lot of the crazy things (and crazy people) in his environment. By also making him smart, rational and sane, he is in constant conflict as he finds creative ways to cope with the craziness and get his show made. He

BaL EPISODE 1

https://vimeo.com/47527116

is the classic "fish out of water," struggling to achieve a goal in a topsy-turvy world without letting it make him crazy, too.

In *The Defenders of Stan,* Stan is not only the last guy on earth without superpowers; he was already, by nature, a deeply ordinary guy with a pretty boring life. (We can see this in the blandness of his clothes, apartment and work cubicle.) If he was a brilliant scientist, famous artist or accomplished ladies' man, he'd suffer less because the difference between him and the superheroes wouldn't be as painfully humiliating; he could simply say, "Well, my life has been pretty awesome so far, no need to worry about not having powers." The central question—"Can Stan find any kind of happiness in a world where he's been left behind?"—wouldn't have much force behind it. By highlighting the mundane, ordinary life Stan is leading, the writers make sure we really feel the pain of Stan's struggle.

Notice that we are looking at two different kinds of "hero" here: the unwilling and the willing. Stan has no choice in his situation; he is living in a world where he is defined as a loser, and his struggle is to live his life with a measure of dignity and satisfaction. In contrast, David Penn could give up and go home, but he chooses to stay and struggle in his environment because he has a goal. Either way, each character has a personality that makes his situation harder. That's no accident. It's good premise and character design that generates conflict, struggle and suffering. It's an almost sadistic task, creating characters who have real feelings only to place them in situations where they'll suffer every minute. But where's the story if everyone's happy and things are going fine and nothing needs to change?

Keep in mind that their suffering needs to be a special kind of struggle. You need characters whose struggle is big enough to keep them plugging away at it episode after episode. So if you want to write a show about your friends or roommates or coworkers, go for it, but keep testing your premise and your central question. Keep checking that your character is designed for maximum suffering and struggle within the environment and situations you create. Focus on your central question and keep asking yourself, "Why does the audience care?" Ultimately, you're creating these characters so that your show works as a whole, has energy and movement and elicits a genuine response in your audience.

Secondary Characters

Not even the most fascinating and cleverly developed character can carry a show by himself, herself or itself. Without other characters to interact with, be "triggered" by, and be revealed through, there's no hope of a story. Here are some of the most common categories of useful secondary characters.

Mirror

Many sitcoms and dramas that you've seen include characters who are clearly designed as *opposites* of the main character. This is the classic "odd couple" dynamic: two people who couldn't be more different constantly annoy each other. Not only does the friction between these characters keep things lively, but the mirror character deepens our understanding of the main character by acting the opposite and providing a contrast. For example, in *Roommates*, Harry and Ted mirror each other; their polar-opposite feelings about Google highlight the dangers and foibles of their respective points of view. In *Coach*, the main character's torment and despair are contrasted with and magnified by Brandon's innocence and hope. In *Friends*, Monica and Phoebe mirror each other as opposites, as do Chandler and Joey. In *Frasier*, the title character is mirrored by his blue-collar, ex-cop father as an opposite; he is also mirrored by Niles, his even more stuffy and overly sophisticated brother, as a contrast on the opposite end of the scale.

Mirror characters can also deepen our understanding of the main character by acting even more extremely "like" the main character, thus providing a *contrast of scale*. In *Dr. Horrible's Singalong Blog*, the sidekick, Moist, is even less evil than the doctor; he's likeable but absolutely pathetic as a superhero. Moist reveals just how low on the scale of evil Dr. Horrible is, and at the same time creates opportunities for the doctor to demonstrate what skills he does have (contrast of scale).

The dramatic function of the mirror character is to illuminate the main character for the audience. It is also sometimes to illuminate the main character to himself or herself. The main character might see his or her own behavior, attitudes, values, etc., in the mirror character and learn an important lesson. Or the main character might remain oblivious to the similarity, while the audience fully grasps the significance.

Foil

Foil characters exist to highlight some aspect of the main character through difference, but not necessarily as an opposite. Instead, they present a kind of commentary on the main character. Foil characters create opportunities for the main character to demonstrate himself or herself: a kid brother who gets picked on at school allows the big sister character to demonstrate protectiveness, courage, loyalty, strength, etc. In *Dr. Horrible's Singalong Blog,* Penny, who is the doctor's love interest, provides a foil by activating his innate goodness (just as he's trying to accomplish a League-worthy feat of evil). When she tries to get him to sign a petition to build a homeless shelter and he reveals his sinister intent to take over the world, her interrogation leads him to acknowledge (inwardly, as well as outwardly) that he doesn't truly want to do harm. We also see his sweet, vulnerable side as he tries to play it cool but can't hide his crush on Penny. At the end of the episode, when his evil plan is thwarted by superhero Captain Hammer, Dr. Horrible berates Captain Hammer not for "saving the day" but for endangering Penny (whom he "saves" by violently tossing her onto a pile of garbage); the evil doctor cares more about her than he does about his evil plan. Thus Penny's character serves to deepen our understanding of Dr. Horrible's inner conflict and complexity.

In a really tight script, every incidental character might serve as a foil, in addition to whatever minor plot role he or she plays. As long as you're giving screen time to that waitress or traffic cop or innocent bystander, why not make the scene work extra hard and use him or her to reinforce something about your main character? For instance, in the pilot episode of *The Defenders of Stan,* Stan's date at first seems to be a kindred spirit, a person without superpowers who actually feels okay about not having them. She offers Stan more hope than most dates do; in her, Stan might have found the cure for his basic internal conflict—his feeling of being left behind. The date says everything Stan has been desperately telling himself and desperately needs to hear from someone else. Then the terrible moment comes: as she reaches for the salt, it slides across the table to her. They both realize she has gained the superpower of telekinesis. She is elated; Stan is dejected.

The dramatic function of this foil character (the date) is to let Stan *show us* how and why he suffers. He is lonely and frustrated about his situation; hope appears in the form of an attractive woman who not only shares Stan's "handicap" but celebrates her unaltered humanity. But this hope is snatched away when she attains powers and immediately forgets all about Stan. Foil characters are created for this purpose; they might be funny or unpleasant or friendly or hostile, but they generate opportunities for the main character to show us what's going on inside.

Antagonists: Tormentor, Threat, Rival

Antagonist characters help clarify what the main character is up against by personifying the forces allied against him or her. In other words, the main character's worst nightmares are made manifest in the person of, say, a tormentor, a rival or a threat. In this way, the drama is both external (in the form of the antagonist) and internal (in the main character's own fears, weaknesses, vulnerabilities).

Tormentor

In *The Defenders of Stan,* we know that Stan's internal conflict is his loneliness and his sense of being left out. He doesn't think he is an inferior person, per se, and he doesn't actually believe that superpowers make anyone better than anyone else. But because he doesn't have those superpowers, he is forced to live with a kind of inferiority he doesn't even believe in. His suffering begins with an external reality (superheroes all around) but culminates in an internal conflict (the unhappiness of being unfairly excluded).

This sense of unfairness is really the sticking point for Stan. He knows he's a good person who doesn't deserve this extra "handicap." He doesn't deserve to be patronized or forgotten because he's different. So how can the writers emphasize the sting of that unfairness? Easy: assign it to an antagonist character. This means to make the antagonist character represent the exact quality or force behind the main character's internal conflict.

In *The Defenders of Stan,* this character is Ted, or Captain Ultra, Stan's brother. As soon as he beams into Stan's living room, we understand how big a drag Stan's life really is—his own brother is not only the world's most popular and beloved superhero, but he's also a total jerk. He's conceited, rude, insulting and inescapable. This is the very essence of a tormentor; everything that irks and troubles Stan—the very core of his suffering—is epitomized in this horrible person, his own brother.

Rival

You've also seen plenty of *rival* characters. These are people who are after the main character's love interest or job, or whose abilities make the main character feel endangered and insecure.

To be dramatically effective, the rival needs to have the power to make the character suffer both external and internal conflicts. If the rival is after the main character's job, then he or she should be clearly capable of getting the job—and in a way that will be especially hurtful for the main character. The main character should suffer not only the loss of the job (external), but a sense of humiliation and having been defeated in more than a material way (internal).

In *Dr. Horrible's Singalong Blog,* the rival character is Captain Hammer, the egotistical superhero who is everything the doctor isn't: confident, powerful and studly. Although Captain Hammer is strong enough to stop evil by brute force, he is also clumsy and somewhat inept, which only adds to Dr. Horrible's humiliation at being defeated by him. And of course, at the end of the episode he steals the girl.

Threat

Main characters are always being threatened: by society, by the people around them, by their own frailties. A threat character is one who has the power to seriously harm the main character. This character may

LY EPISODE 2

or may not wish to harm anyone, but he or she definitely has the power to. Andy Corvell in *Leap Year* is an example. He holds the fragile psyche (and finances) of the main character, Aaron, in his hands. His potential threat is clear and imminent: he can, and probably will, fire Aaron (and all of his friends to boot). What makes Andy work is that he doesn't try to seem powerful; his shtick is to be the empowering, supportive, caring nurturer-on-steroids. His actual nature, and power, come out in his off-the-cuff remarks, which reveal what a dangerous and capricious nutcase he really is. This feeds into

Aaron's external dramatic need (to keep his job) and his internal need (to feel a shred of safety in his job, and hence his life). Andy Corvell is profoundly threatening in both areas.

THE STORY WORLD

Characters need catalysts for action; they need a location, setting or other characters that constantly push their buttons. Think of your show as a lab experiment in which your characters are placed in a controlled setting designed to produce constant drama and conflict. This controlled setting is your *story world.*

Your story world isn't simply a location or a setting where the characters interact. It's a very specific type of container for your drama; it sets the tone of your show. Imagine if *The Office* were set in a cosmopolitan ad agency like the one in *Mad Men*. Both shows treat themes of corporate life, but the settings (time and place) make the shows completely different. The themes of depressing, dead-end office work and of corporate structures that keep smart people down would be lost if the setting were the posh Manhattan offices of Sterling Cooper, where powerful men compete for high stakes and fantastic rewards. Or imagine if *Mad Men* were set in the dreary Dunder–Mifflin building in Scranton, Pennsylvania. Besides the obvious aesthetic difference, what would happen to the themes of decadence, glamour and unfettered ambition? What range of actions and desires could the characters have in that environment? Would the show still have its distinct sense of nostalgia and social critique? The story world largely dictates the story possibilities.

Pacing the Explanation

Audiences like to have things fleshed out, so they can be immersed in an imaginary realm. This is true of TV and also online video; but in the online format that rich understanding is based on detail that is chosen more carefully and delivered more efficiently.

In *The Defenders of Stan*, the story world looks like the world we live in, except that nearly everyone on the planet is gaining superpowers. If you had created this show, you might have considered building in some backstory to explain how the world got that way. Did some kind of mutant virus-carrying asteroid hit Earth? Was a latent superhero gene activated in humans by environmental changes?

In a film or TV series, this question would be answered at some length, probably early in the film or pilot episode. The writers would be careful to avoid moving the story forward too much without giving the audience a solid understanding of the world; considerable time would be spent making sure the audience had enough background information to feel comfortable about how things got the way they are in the story world.

In online video, you don't have that kind of time. The good news is that not only do you need to keep things shorter, but you have more leeway to do so. You can trust the audience to accept weird realities without a lot of explanation. This is a major (and delightful) difference between TV and online shows: TV audiences are familiar and comfortable with a narrow range of genres, whereas online audiences are accustomed to watching strange, idiosyncratic content that doesn't always stick with those conventions.

A good example is *The Parent Project* (www.youtube.com/watch? v=3MAi1OMH7bI), which opens with titles reading: "This month, I called my mom to get a Channel 101 show idea. These are excerpts from those conversations." Next, we hear the show creator talking to his mom, who does indeed suggest a storyline. As she describes the characters and events, the show cuts to a dramatic reenactment of the story. Each episode features this combination of phone conversations and dramatic scenes. Along the way, we get a delightful dose of meta-story as we hear the mother, who is clearly not an experienced writer, become more and more involved with the plot and characters, while her son ignores his own storytelling sense and good-naturedly makes the show exactly as she dictates. The quirky relationship between mother and son and the tangents of their conversations create an extra level of interest. Such a show probably wouldn't make it on TV because it ventures into an odd format and fails to deliver the expected markers of a genre. However, *The Parent Project* had a long and popular run and is listed in many "greatest online show" compendiums.

Online audiences expect things to move quickly and are able to fill in some blanks as they watch. They accept a given reality and do not worry much about the explanation, at least for a while. The trick is to figure out how much "filling in blanks" you can ask the audience to do, and for how long.

When you're designing your story world, you might find you have a lot of explaining to do with regard to a time shift, a supernatural or metaphysical abnormality, alternate history, maybe even straightforward science fiction. You, of course, will know everything there is to know about your story world—but does your audience have to? A big part of your job right now is to decide (a) what information the audience needs right away; (b) what you can "marble" in; and (c) and what you can leave out altogether. How do you decide?

First, select the information

One rule is absolute: Give the audience whatever they need to understand the scene they're seeing right now. Imagine for a moment that you are not allowed to explain anything about your story world beyond what the audience needs to understand each scene as it occurs. Understanding a scene means knowing a character well enough to see why he or she responds in a certain way to an event or another character. This kind of understanding doesn't have to be supplemented by a lot of backstory; in fact, the scene will have greater impact if it stays focused on the emotional or psychological drama rather than exposition. If the audience understands what is going on with the character right now, they are engaged and can wait for the "big picture" to be fully explained.

Possibly, the "big picture" is never fully explained. You should never deprive the audience of understanding what your story world is like, but you don't necessarily have to explain why it is that way, or how it got that way. In *The Defenders of Stan,* we don't actually learn what happened to the world or why suddenly everyone is gaining superpowers. Why not? Is that important to know?

Watch the pilot episode again, especially focusing on the opening scenes. Do you feel hung up on wondering how the story world got that way? Or can you follow what is going on in each scene, based on what you learn about Stan as events unfold?

In the first two scenes, Stan's frowning reaction to the superheroes populating his reality tells us everything we need to know to understand the drama: he is living in an unpleasant reality and is already tired of it. Instead of getting caught up in explaining what happened to the world, the scene focuses on the themes of abandonment and loneliness. In fact, we never learn in this episode how the world came to be populated by superheroes. There is no backstory and no given explanation. We are shown what the reality is and given a character to relate to, and the story begins. We know everything we need to understand what's going on with Stan; we grasp the emotional and psychological drama of each scene. In a way, part of the fun is going along with the premise without having it explained; such an explanation might actually "break the spell." It certainly would make the series feel more like conventional TV. The premise of *The Defenders of Stan* isn't necessarily too weird for television, but the show feels more original and quirky than TV. This is partly because of the playful way we are asked to jump right in and participate in the shared fiction, rather than waiting for backstory and explanation.

Obviously, while you can leave out more than you might have thought, you don't want to deprive the audience of anything essential to understanding your story world and the drama unfolding within it. The question now is when and how to deliver that knowledge. For instance, the job of the first scene of *The Defenders of Stan* (http://ny.channel101.com/view.php?epid=176) is to illustrate not just the reality of the story world, but—equally importantly—its meaning for the main character. We need to understand that Stan is depressed and frustrated with the situation. We don't yet need to know all the facts about the story world; diluting the "ouch" of the first scene would deprive it of its emotional energy and weaken the drama.

Similarly, the second scene featuring Stan's coworker Blue could have been used to flesh out Blue's character, or even to develop Stan's character by giving him a sympathetic listener. We could have heard Stan articulate his feelings to his co-worker; perhaps the co-worker would have promised to be Stan's friend and keep him from being left out, or perhaps he would offer information about a medical procedure that could help Stan develop powers. These would be interesting developments, but again, they would undermine the drama by prematurely solving the central question of the show, which is about Stan's life of loneliness. So the first scenes are strictly about establishing a clear polarity between Stan and the rest of the world. We are given as many facts as we need—or rather, as Stan needs to react to. We, the audience, don't need to process a lot to understand how he feels, because in each scene the writers stay focused on the job at hand.

What other facts about the story world might you have been tempted to introduce as backstory, or explain earlier in the episode? We learn that Captain Ultra is Stan's brother, and that their parents died of cancer. Would any of this information have improved the audience's grasp of the drama in the first scenes? Or would it simply have been distracting clutter?

Then decide when to reveal

Deciding when to reveal information can be tricky. Beyond the rule of giving the audience whatever they need to understand each scene as it unfolds, how does a writer know when or how to develop the "big picture"?

The term *marbling* describes how such information can be distributed throughout the script, rather than in big chunks of exposition that slow the story down or clutter up your scenes. Recall Blue's monologue in the office scene in *The Defenders of Stan*. As he chats away, he drops some facts about the story world, including that superheroes comprise 93 percent of the population now and Jerry Seinfeld now has bones made of rubber. These facts arise naturally in this familiar scenario of a talkative co-worker loitering around a desk; the writers slip the information in while writing an entertaining and believable exchange between the characters.

Later, Captain Ultra materializes in Stan's apartment and calls him "little brother." He accuses Stan of feeling guilty that he couldn't save their parents; Stan replies, "What? From cancer?" All of this information comes to us at points in the story when it is useful and when it can arise naturally in the scene. We didn't get it before we needed it. In fact, some of it we didn't even need; it doesn't really matter to the series that Stan's parents died of cancer. That might have been part of the writers' conception of their story world, but there was no need for the audience to know it earlier, and if it hadn't been part of a useful exchange between characters—an exchange that effectively characterizes the bully/bullied relationship between Stan and his brother—it might never have been mentioned at all.

A good way to practice marbling is to identify everything in your script that is an objective or factual explanation of your story world, and temporarily lift it out. What's left will be your characters' internal dramatic need. When you come to places in the script where your characters' emotional responses don't make sense, it's likely that something about the story world needs to be explained. That's when you decide what minimum information is required, and marble it in, a little at a time.

Setting Boundaries

Your story world might not have any supernatural or metaphysical components, but it is nevertheless a fictional world, one that you are constructing specifically to generate drama around a set of characters. It isn't simply "the real world" as each audience member knows it, so you have to introduce us to it and teach us about it as we go along.

This happens very naturally in *The Parent Project* as Mom narrates the story to her son, explaining the characters and their relationships, and as we see the dramatic reenactment, which adds clarity and definition to the story we've just heard told. In addition, another story world comes into focus: the one inhabited by mother and son. We aren't given background information about them, and we don't know their family history, but their conversation reveals a world unto itself.

It might not be vastly different from the world we all share, but nevertheless it is one that we don't occupy and can only know through the information we receive as we watch.

In *Leap Year,* we meet a group of characters who live in a world we recognize as normal. But we don't see the whole world in this show; we see a carefully constructed slice of it—a fictional reality that includes particular people and cultural themes. Specifically, we see people in their late 20s navigating a cultural climate of corporate collapse, economic uncertainty and entrepreneurial opportunity. Because these are all recognizable realities, especially to the audience who will most relate to the characters and premise of the show, it might seem that the writers don't have to worry about establishing the rules of the story world. But they do, just as if they were writing science fiction or fantasy.

Like nearly all story worlds, the story world of *Leap Year* consists of particular locations. Notice what these are, and what and whom we see the most. The pilot episode begins with Aaron and Lisa on a romantic birthday date; it ends with them together in their bed. We also see them walking alone through the city, and alone in small spaces such as stairwells and porches. We are brought physically very close to these characters and into their personal, intimate space.

We also see Aaron's group of friends together at a bar and at his birthday party. Again, we are close to the characters and feel their camaraderie. This story world is an intimate one; its natural boundary

LY EPISODE 1

https://vimeo.com/47871716

is the couple and their friends who function as a family. Threats and dangers will come from the outside world. Notice how "the outside world" is simply the world we all live in today and how distinctly the writers have defined their story world and differentiated it from the real world. The story world isn't actually different; it's just highly focused.

Co-authors Yuri and Vlad on creating a story world

Here's what Yuri and Vlad Baranovsky, co-authors of this book and the creators of Leap Year *and* Break a Leg, *have to say about creating a story world:*

First, make some firm decisions about the rules and structure of your world. Once established, you have to Keep It Consistent, Stupid (the KICS principle)—if you've correctly laid out the world and its laws in the first episode, the rest of the season must use the same rules. Yes, they can adapt and evolve, but if episode 2 has flying blue people when the first episode followed the real world misadventures of café workers, your viewers will think you're either a bad writer or schizophrenic.

Every show has its world and each world has its own lore, its own characters and, most importantly, its own rules. *Break a Leg*'s world consisted of a bizarro Hollywood where child actors lived in the sewers and the trade unions were in actual war with one another. It also had its unspoken rules—for example, while the *plot* was entirely silly and over-the-top, the *characters* functioned within the limitations of the real world. No one could fly, no one could teleport and most everything could be explained with real-world mechanics—even if the explanation was often as silly as the actual event.

Establishing your world also means figuring out the genre of your story. Is it a romantic comedy? Is it a drama? Is it sci-fi? Keeping consistent with the genre means keeping consistent with the rules of your world. If your pilot episode is a romantic comedy that takes place in the real world, it would be very jarring if aliens showed up in episode 8 and Will Smith had to stop them. In many ways, knowing the genre—be it something straightforward like sci-fi, or more experimental like a comedy-space-Western—gives you a strong framework of rules that you can then build your world on.

Don't despair at the words *rules* and *genre*. Your creativity doesn't need to be stifled by narrative conventions; in fact, most writers find that articulating some basic show parameters really helps focus on the clarity and impact of the story. And every story doesn't have to be a neat and tidy narrative of events in chronological order—but it should invite us to engage with a character and a crisis in a particular setting. Think of the greatest, most original and powerful and unique story you've ever read, or the greatest play or TV show or film you've seen. Are any of the above elements missing? See if you can identify the "hot spots" where your brain signals you to pay attention, to be curious or interested, to care, to find meaning. And yes, laughter is definitely a sign of finding meaning.

Read, watch or listen to the piece again and ask yourself: Who am I paying the most attention to right now? What's happening to them, and why does it matter? What are they doing in response? You'll find that there's a strong connection between who the characters are, and what kinds of things are happening to them or around them. Again, this is because the writers deliberately created a world that would *especially* trouble and provoke *those characters.*

Perhaps you're thinking, "But if my characters are really funny, the jokes will carry the show. I don't need to build around a story." If so, stop reading right now and go find an online video that you like, that you think works without story. Ignore the "drunk cats on skateboards/flushing the toilet/singing with the radio" category of user-generated content; find shows that were scripted and produced as series or coherent bodies of work. One excellent source for this exercise is the "Failed Pilots" section on the Channel 101 site (www.channel101.com) and the Channel 101 New York site (http://ny.channel101.com). Notice which ones seem like something that you would tune into regularly, that arouse your interest, and which ones strike you as lacking something, perhaps a bit flat, boring, or confusing, or hard to get into; you might watch a few minutes but soon you get tired of the joke and move on. Without characters who are struggling with a central question in a world designed to challenge them, the piece might be briefly amusing but fail to interest you in returning for more episodes.

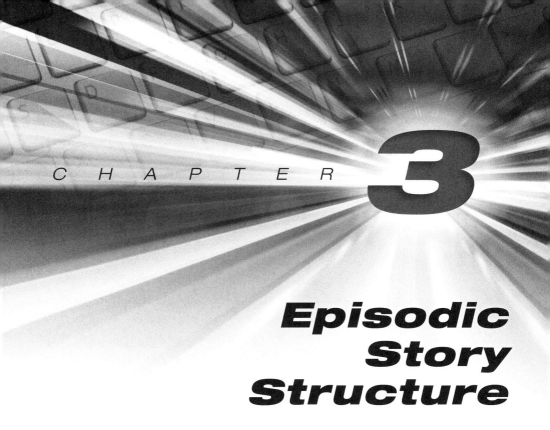

3

Episodic Story Structure

You've probably heard of three-act structure: stories that have a beginning, a middle and an end. Aristotle first analyzed and articulated this as basic "dramatic structure," but he didn't invent it. It evolved out of the way our brains process information and organize experience into systems of meaning. Our earliest myths and legends follow this structure. Novelists, dramatists, poets, essayists and speechwriters have always used it. Audiences generally expect and respond to it. In fact, they often expect and require it. If a story feels confusing, boring or pointless, it's likely that a structural element is weak or missing.

Storytelling is really a way of guiding the audience through an imaginary experience: pushing the right button at the right time to elicit particular responses (curiosity, sympathy, indignation, amusement, horror, desire, suspense, relief, etc.). For this imaginary experience to work, the audience needs to get the pieces of the story in the right order. You'll encounter a variety of terms for these elements, but their functions are simple and clear. Here we'll call them the *setup, rising action* and *resolution.*

THE SETUP

For screenwriters, structure is a useful way to track what's happening to the audience at each stage of the story: What information they are receiving, what psychological and emotional cues they are responding to and what significance they are attaching to the events of the story as it unfolds. Of the three parts, the *setup* is the most crucial section of your script. This is where you establish the characters, motivations and plot of your story. It is where you hook the audience into becoming curious, concerned and engaged. Without a strong setup, the audience will not have a sufficient grasp of who your characters are, what is happening to them, what they are doing about it or *why any of it matters.* In other words, without a strong setup, you'll have an episode that feels flat.

The setup is given in the first scene, or sequence of scenes, of an episode. In just a few minutes, the audience should be shown three things:

1. A character with some easily identifiable qualities, wants and needs.
2. A problem that arises.
3. How the character has no choice but to try to solve the problem.

Chapter 1 talked about creating a controlled story world for your characters, and Chapter 4 will discuss designing characters that will generate and thrive on conflict. In your episode setup, your job is to shake up the character's world with a specific problem, or *crisis,* that the character cannot escape or ignore. This crisis will compel him or her to struggle for an entire episode.

The crisis can also be called a "change in the status quo." It means that we enter the story just as the normal state of things is being *significantly disrupted,* and the main character is placed in a situation to which he or she *must respond.*

This strategic combination generates the tension that gives the audience a sense of engagement with and concern about the character. The audience must clearly understand why *this* situation is especially compelling (threatening, frightening, tempting, etc.) for *this* character. It doesn't matter whether the situation is life-or-death or something most people would consider trivial: knowing what we know about *this character,* we understand *why* he or she is driven to respond. That drive must be strong enough—and clear enough in the script—to sustain a whole episode's worth of struggle, conflict and triumph or defeat.

In a half-hour TV sitcom, the setup might take three or four minutes. Short-format episodes must get the same job done in much less time, sometimes even less than one minute. To accomplish this, the traditional setup form has been streamlined; often, a short-format episode will skip establishing a status quo and begin in the middle of the crisis. For example, the pilot episode of *Coach* opens with the first tragic accidental killing, and the main character abandoning his life and going on the run. In the first few minutes of *Dr. Horrible's Singalong Blog,* we learn that the main character is anxiously awaiting a response to his application to the Evil League of Evil. *Leap Year* begins with Aaron in a state of fear and turmoil about his endangered career. We don't see what his life was like before this state of panic; we don't see a status quo and then see it disrupted. From the first second, we see the story world and the character already in crisis. In both cases, we are brought into the story already in progress; the information we need about character backgrounds, the story world, etc., is revealed as the episode continues.

LY EPISODE 1

https://vimeo.com/47871716

Assuming that your show will consist of many episodes, you're going to spend a lot of time coming up with crises and situations. You might draw inspiration from your own life, from current events, from things you read and watch, etc. Always be on the lookout for a good situation! But keep in mind that no situation is complete unless it *connects to the show's central question.* No problem, challenge or crisis, however dramatic, is going to feel compelling in *The Defenders of Stan* unless it connects to the central question of Stan finding a way to be less lonely, or in *Leap Year* unless it connects to Aaron's deep fear of failure and the loss of his happy family life. For every crisis you think of, ask yourself whether it addresses your show's central question; if it doesn't, see if you can adjust it so it does. If you can't, or if it starts to seem too contrived, put it in the "save for later" file and move on to a different situation. Your audience will thank you.

The setup is where you lay the groundwork for the conflict your main character will face throughout the rest of the episode. The audience learns about the character's fears, weaknesses, vulnerabilities, quirks, mannerisms, habits and attitudes. This knowledge enables us to connect to and empathize with the character, so that as the story unfolds we stay engaged and interested in the outcome. The setup, of course, is only the beginning. What you build upon that foundation is the bulk of the story.

The goal of the setup is to drive your main character into action; in other words, it kicks off the story.

RISING ACTION

In a sense, action is simply plot: the logical sequence of events in your story, or what happens. But *rising action* is a dramatic term that refers to the emotional and psychological tension driving your story.

Once your character has experienced a disruption of the status quo and has been spurred into action, the rest of the story consists of his or her attempts to solve the problem. These attempts might be risky and dangerous, or silly and hilarious. Whatever they are, in dramatic terms they're called *struggle*. Your episode is the story of a character's struggle to solve a problem.

What is the character struggling against? This could be a lot of things: bad luck, tornadoes, a giant flying shark. But your character's most compelling struggles will be with other people and with his or her own limitations. Just as you designed a crisis suited to your character, you will design struggles that compel your character, relate to your show's central question and reflect the tone and style of your show.

Obstacles and Conflict

Obviously, a struggle requires an obstacle—something that stands between the character and his or her goal. Obstacles can be external or internal. External obstacles often serve to delay or derail the character's progress: a traffic jam; a car that won't start; a chatty neighbor who knows something important but won't get to the point, thus preventing the character from dashing off to fix the crisis. External obstacles are great for building a sense of frustration and for emphasizing a time-lock (a ticking bomb, a date waiting at the restaurant, a boss threatening to fire the character for being tardy). They are also generic and fairly arbitrary; they could happen to anyone.

To avoid this sense of arbitrariness, make sure your character responds to the external obstacle in a way that is unique to him or her. Even the most random events can be opportunities to reveal and reinforce your character's basic nature. Perhaps the obstacle is something that could happen to anyone, but not everyone would respond how your character does.

Even so, an episode that only features external obstacles might feel shallow, boring or even slapstick, because such obstacles tend to be quickly overcome so that the character can move on to the next phase of the story.

Internal obstacles reveal more about the character. Perhaps he or she struggles against a phobia, a crushing sense of inferiority or chronic forgetfulness. These all bring us closer to the character, helping to activate our compassion or empathy. However, notice that internal obstacles are all part of a character's basic nature—the character struggles against them *all the time*. Internal obstacles need to be established clearly and early in a series so that when they are triggered by a situation, we aren't learning about them for the first time. Both types of obstacles are useful but rather one-sided: the character against something circumstantial, or against him/herself in a general, ongoing way. What's missing? To create a really meaningful, compelling struggle that will keep the audience engaged with your character, think in terms of *conflict*. Obstacles are things to be overcome. Conflict is a process of engagement that requires your character to face the same adversary in a range of circumstances, to draw on all of his or her abilities, to suffer from failure and to learn from it. Your character learns about him/herself through conflict, and so does the audience.

External conflict

Conflict, like obstacles, can be external or internal. External conflict happens between characters. This is a very rich form of conflict, because it encompasses the full range of human experience: love, hate, envy, contempt, resentment, admiration, disappointment, impossible expectations. Every feeling that has ever passed between two people can be a source of conflict in your story, and your audience will feel it as strongly as your characters.

The important thing to remember here is that *feelings aren't story*. There's no story until there's a conflict. Your character might have a crush on a co-worker, but there's no conflict until something happens. The character must work up the courage to ask the co-worker out, or he unwisely confides in the office blabbermouth or he convinces a friend to woo the co-worker via email. Somehow you have to get both sides involved; the character and someone who has the power to affect the situation for better or worse must interact. This might be the source of the character's feelings (the co-worker) or someone else involved (the blabbermouth, the friend).

Does external conflict mean that the character has to get in an argument or fight with someone? Not at all. It means people with their own feelings, quirks, egos and agendas play a part in the main character's struggle. These people can be in conflict with the main character simply by being themselves. When the office blabbermouth tells the co-worker about the main character's crush, there could be a confrontation or we may never see the blabbermouth again.

Of course, direct conflict is an extremely engaging form of drama. Think how juicy a confrontation with the office blabbermouth could be, or a revenge scheme in which the character manages to expose and humiliate the blabbermouth. We love watching people fight. It's a primal instinct. Think about the sports we watch and the video games we play; think about all the movies and shows you've watched and the songs you've listened to that are based on someone's anger, unrequited love or jealousy toward someone else (and what happened as a result). Because direct conflict is such a powerful dramatic element, you will want to use your show's secondary characters and perhaps design new ones in specific episodes to conflict with your main character and to keep that "fight" energy alive in your show.

Conflict can also occur between your character and the world around him or her. In *The Defenders of Stan* (http://ny.channel101. com/view.php?epid=176). Stan is constantly in conflict with the reality that everyone around him has powers. That, of course, is the central question of the show. Can Stan come to terms with this reality? But conflict can't just exist in the form of a character's strong feelings; it has to manifest in something we can see happen. Each episode must present *visible, dramatic instances* of this ongoing conflict. For example, on Stan's big date, he asks the question that underscores his whole life: "Why don't we have powers? What's holding us back?" His date offers Stan hope at first; she doesn't care about not having powers. Then she reaches for the salt, and it magically slides across the table. She has just gained telekinesis and shrieks with joy and excitement, while Stan hangs his head in dismay and signals for the check.

In this instance, Stan's conflict with his world manifests in an incident with a foil character (the date). Stan (a) experiences a betrayal; (b) suffers a complication of his problem or quest (the destruction of that one glimmer of hope); and (c) is forced to face the fact that the whole mess stems from his inability to accept his situation, and so he faces his own continuing misery.

Internal conflict

Stan's conflict with the world is also a kind of internal conflict. The problem exists outside of Stan, so it is in part external. But Stan also faces an internal conflict with himself: he wants to accept his situation so that he can stop suffering over it, and he knows he has to do that; but at the same time, he desperately hopes that he *will* get powers. It is important that this internal struggle be made visible. The audience can't see or hear wishes, hopes, fears or any other feelings until actions or dialogue reveal them. In this instance, we see Stan's internal struggle when he insists to his brother that he's okay with not having powers, but moments later sits down at his kitchen table and tries, hoping against hope, to make his saltshaker move toward him. That is an internal struggle made visible through character action. Internal conflicts create intimate knowledge of characters, particularly of their vulnerabilities—which tend to build audience sympathy and concern for the character. It is a heartrending moment when Stan, after being taunted by his superhero brother, succumbs to his deep wish to be like everyone else and tries to make that saltshaker move. We know he won't succeed; we are engaged not through suspense but through pity.

Escalating Tension

As the seconds and minutes tick by in your episode, your main character will face a range of internal and external obstacles and will try to overcome them. This journey must have a sense of movement toward something. This movement is a key component of rising action. If you were to graph the scale and significance of the events of the story in the order that they occur, you would see a steep upward slope with a short downward tag at the end. The upward slope represents an escalation in the tension of the story.

The reason this slope needs to rise upward is that humans are wired to pay attention to stimuli only until they are processed as either dangerous or safe. Once an event (i.e., your character encountering an obstacle or a conflict) is dealt with in your story, your audience stops reacting to it and needs a greater stimulus to return to that attentive state. In other words, your character can't face a medium-sized problem, another medium-sized problem, then a small problem and another small problem. This feels like a flatlining story, because the stimuli for the audience remain constant or weaken. For example, in *Coach* (http://www.channel101.com/episode/953) the main character's dramatic need is to redeem himself by successfully coaching someone who needs his help. He encounters *increasing* obstacles as, first, his own trauma nearly prevents him from coaching Brandon into using his car's brakes; second, Brandon learns that Coach had initially planned to kill him and steal his car and rejects him; and finally, at the moment of final triumph, as Coach gives his most motivating speech, Brandon dies of a brain aneurism. Tension rises as it becomes less and less likely that Coach will succeed. However, if the writers had interrupted the steep upward slope of the tension graph by dropping in some less significant obstacles—say Brandon's car gets a flat and Coach has to teach him how to change a tire, just as he had coached him into braking a few minutes earlier, and they go on their way—the story would have suffered from a drop in energy because the real obstacles would have taken a back seat to an unimportant problem that was quickly solved. You want the tension to steadily strengthen, creating more and more "ouch" as the minutes of your story pass.

One strategy for achieving this is known as *raising the stakes* for your character. When you establish your show's premise and central question, you are giving your character a dramatic need. It can be something concrete, such as a successful career switch, or something emotional or psychological, such as relief from feeling excluded from the world. (Hopefully, you have given your character both external and internal needs.) This need points to what is *at stake* for your character: his or her financial security, mental and emotional well-being and so on.

Each obstacle and conflict in your story should clearly indicate what is at stake in that scene, present a clear threat to it and remind us of how much it means to the character. This is raising the stakes. In the pilot episode of *Leap Year,* the setup at Aaron's birthday dinner tells us what is at stake for him. Externally, he wants financial security; internally, he wants relief from his chronic terror that everything is on the verge of falling apart. As the episode progresses, each scene or sequence will present a tangible threat to Aaron's dramatic needs, each one greater than the last.

For example, in the next sequence Aaron's co-workers invoke one of Aaron's major fears: he bought his wife a pregnancy whistle the minute he found out she was pregnant because he's afraid she'll go into early labor and have the baby in the street. At the same time, his friends are speculating about an ominous "all-hands" meeting at their company. Aaron jumps immediately to the thought that there are going to be layoffs. Now his generalized fear of losing his job with a baby on the way has been made concrete. The scene introduces a tangible threat to his financial security. Then, as if Aaron weren't already suffering enough, his brother comes along and, hearing about

Dramatic arcs within dramatic arcs

Even sequences have their own dramatic arc. First, the setup in which Aaron's fear is invoked and a hint is dropped about an ominous meeting; second, the action (news of the meeting, Aaron articulating the immediate threat of layoffs); and finally, an escalation (the brother's remark about Lisa not being pregnant) that reinforces the internal dramatic need of the main character. As you're writing your script, be constantly on the lookout for opportunities to escalate tension both in individual scenes/sequences and in the episode as a whole. Is your character facing a barking dog? Make the dog and the situation scarier. You could plant an earlier reference to the character's fear of dogs or give the dog rabies. Is the conflict between a couple who is breaking up? Make the situation worse by creating a "time lock," for instance, a friend's upcoming wedding or other occasion where going dateless would be humiliating. The idea is to make your characters' struggles hard in as many ways as possible.

the layoffs, says it's a good thing Lisa isn't pregnant. There's the increased "ouch." The news that layoffs are a possibility is naturally a tension-filled event, and would serve nicely on its own as an obstacle for Aaron. But the writers go a step further and increase the tension of the scene by first invoking the larger fear to remind us what is emotionally at stake for Aaron, and then presenting the immediate threat to his job, thus framing the threat in the context of his bigger fears.

Later scenes ramp up the stakes further, pushing the threat level higher and higher:

LY EPISODE 1

https://vimeo.com/47871716

1. Lisa begs Aaron to stop talking about the pregnancy as if it were the worst news in the world. This raises a deeper internal conflict, that Aaron is letting his fear blind him to the happiness in his life right now, which returns us to the central question of the show: Will Aaron learn to transcend his fear and embrace the fullness of this life?

LY EPISODE 1

2. Aaron's co-worker argues that the layoffs are really an opportunity, a catalyst for all of them to do what they've dreamed of for years, which is to start their own businesses. Now there's a huge "at stake" on the table, and Aaron is pushed to take a huge risk. Again, the writers frame this new threat in the context of Aaron's greater internal conflict by having him protest that he's got a baby on the way and shouldn't be taking such risks.

3. The next-to-final sequence of the episode delivers the strongest example of dramatic need vs. threat.

LY EPISODE 1

It opens with an exchange between Aaron and Lisa that is intimate and companionable, but also has an element of anger on Lisa's

LY EPISODE 1

part. She is taking a stand and forcing him to drop his neurosis for her sake. If Aaron doesn't lighten up, she's going to start interpreting his behavior as a rejection of her efforts and affection. Now there's even more at stake; the easy friendliness of their relationship is being threatened.

This strategy of framing external conflict and tangible threats within the context of greater internal needs and connecting them to the show's central question is one that writers rely on constantly. The more opportunities you find to do this, both overtly and subtly, the more engaging your show will feel to the audience.

There are other strategies you can rely on as well. One is to establish the main threat in the setup, and then move it closer and closer to the main character as the story unfolds. This strategy is used to great effect in *The Defenders of Stan* (http://ny.channel101.com/view.php?epid=176). The setup establishes that the greatest threat to Stan is his sense of isolation and being left behind. This threat is manifest three times, each in a specific setting.

1. We see Stan suffer in his workplace. We learn that even Stan's secretary has left for a life of superhero adventure and he is basically alone.

2. Next, we see Stan at a restaurant where he suffers in his social/romantic life. On his big date, he thinks for a moment that he has found a companion and an ally, but when she gains telekinesis he is once again thrust into conflict and threatened with isolation. This is a more intimate venue of suffering than the workplace; here the threat is much *closer* to Stan.

3. Finally, when his obnoxious brother, Captain Ultra, beams into Stan's living room, we see there is nowhere Stan can escape from

his suffering. It pervades even his home and family life. This is, psychologically, the worst expression of the basic threat because it is closest to him—he is in fact completely immersed in it.

Another strategy that helps escalate tension is "tightening the thumbscrews" on your character. Start the story in a tough situation and make that situation tougher as the episode goes on. *Break a Leg* uses this strategy, not only in the structure of the pilot episode but also in the series premise and central question.

RESOLUTION

The upward curve of the graph of your episode culminates in a "do or die" moment, one in which the main character is fully and inescapably committed to overcoming the basic threat, and in which the character is actually in the most danger, both externally and internally. This is the climactic battle between the Rebels and the evil Empire or the fight Rocky has been training for. Everything is at stake in this moment and there can be no surrender or wave of a white flag. The main character has to succeed or fail.

Failure is definitely an option. Every episode doesn't have a happy ending. In *The Defenders of Stan*, Stan fails in his struggle to come to terms with his situation and find contentment in his new life as the only person left without superpowers. When we see him reach across the table for the saltshaker, hoping to find that he too has spontaneously acquired telekinesis, we understand his desperation. It is a moment of ultimate defeat that ends the episode. The answer to the central question of whether Stan will escape his loneliness is a sad and resounding "No." But we don't feel that the whole series is over; the central question has only been answered for this episode. Dramatically, the question has been blown wide open. That moment of failure actually sets up the rest of the series, because now we really understand what is at stake. We will watch the rest of the episodes in a heightened state of attention and concern, which is a great outcome for the writers and for the audience (if not for Stan).

Some resolutions are essentially positive but still feel foreboding, or combine excitement with anxiety. In the closing scene of *Leap Year,* we are returned once more to the intimacy of Aaron and

LY EPISODE 1

Lisa's life together. As they lie in bed, Aaron asks her to say that they'll be okay. When she answers him, we can see that he is trying to believe it—he clearly doesn't, entirely, but he is making a courageous choice to make that leap. This is the peak of the graph, the moment that the whole story was leading up to: the central question of the episode is answered as Aaron makes a can't-go-back commitment at a very deep level. At the same time, the question becomes even bigger and tension is raised because now we need to know whether he will succeed in the larger picture.

Dialogue

Writing dialogue is an art. If you listen to a regular conversation, there is a rhythm, a song, a personality that changes not only from group to group but also from person to person. Your job as a writer is to capture that rhythm in your script, to give life to characters through their words and to give every single person you write about his or her own voice.

Dialogue can sometimes become a secondary concern in an art that relies so heavily on story and structure, but in fact dialogue can make or break your series. In a comedy, the way you choose your words and even the number of words you use can be the difference between a joke that kills (that's good) and a joke that lands flat. In drama, the dialogue can bring your audience to tears and can stick with them for the rest of their lives.

Dialogue is also critical in making your script feel polished and complete. Professional scripts do this well, and that's why they are usually sharp. There's nothing extra, no jokes fall flat, no character arcs remain incomplete, and no strands of plot are left untied. The problem with web shows is that very few feel truly polished, which is one reason why it's hard for the potential sponsors and networks to take the genre seriously.

Dialogue is an issue in the web series genre, as there are very few shows with strong dialogue. There are series with witty dialogue, but it's often missing the structural elements that are key in creating a strong story. The elements above will help you develop all aspects of your character's words, making them not only sound natural but also support the rest of your script.

As a writer, your job is to commit to your dialogue, to craft it as diligently as you craft your plot and characters. This way you can rise above the hundreds of poorly written web shows crowding the Internet and give yours the professional flare that very few have.

Your characters' words will differ greatly depending on a slew of varying elements, which is why it's important to ask yourself several basic questions when writing your dialogue:

- What do I want the dialogue to do?
- Is the show a comedy or a drama?
- What style is the dialogue going to have?

Answering these questions will save you hours of writing (and throwing away) unfocused, meandering dialogue that doesn't move the story.

WHAT IS THE "JOB" OF THE DIALOGUE?

Before you sit down to nail the rhythm and choose just the right words to make people laugh, cry and quote you non-stop, you need to make sure the words actually do something. The dialogue should *serve the story* and *develop character*—both of which tight, hardworking dialogue will do naturally throughout your script. Here are some dialogue rules to keep your lines from being simply a stream of words.

Nothing Extra

As a general rule, a screenplay should contain no extraneous lines; every line should have a purpose. Among the most important functions of dialogue are:

- developing characters whose traits create conflict and contribute to the plot
- foreshadowing future events
- illuminating the story's themes

In practice, this rule is a tiny bit malleable, in that dialogue often contains *banter.* In shows like *Californication* or in many of Judd Apatow's films, the dialogue is filled with banter, but it always serves to reinforce the characters' personalities, which in turn are integral to the story. In *The Parent Project,* the conversation between mother and son wanders across a vast landscape of topics, but there's nothing vague or random about its function: it reveals the mother's lack of experience in writing or analyzing stories, juxtaposed with her exuberant creativity and surprising efforts to take over creative direction of the project. Banter should not be merely tangential. Always ask yourself if your banter is working hard to serve the story. If it's not (and be honest), maybe it's there because you think it's funny; in this case, as painful as it may be, cut it.

In some shows, like *Dr. Horrible's Singalong Blog* and *The Defenders of Stan,* almost all dialogue is in some way brought back in the story. Really tight scripts contain no "fat"; every small moment, every seemingly casual throwaway line comes back as a significant element of the story, whether as a plot element or a revelation about a character's inner struggle. While there's room to play on the continuum from banter to watertight, the "nothing extra" rule should always be your trusted guide.

Subtext

Subtext is information that is suggested but not directly stated by the text. It's the implied meaning of words, and it is a big part of how people interact with one another. Have you ever seen two people who don't like each other—frenemies, perhaps, or reluctant friends-of-friends—have a conversation? It's like a carefully orchestrated, verbal dance-fight that's all based on subtext. Nary a sincere word is spoken. It's all backhanded compliments sandwiched between subtle (yet high-octane and hurtful) jabs: "Jane! I haven't seen you in so long, it's like you dropped off the face of the earth! I love your coat; I can never wear boxy things like that. You look so *tired*, is everything okay? I know a great aesthetician who could fix you right up."

We are constantly using subtext in our day-to-day conversations, and so should our characters. Otherwise, we can end up with "on-the-nose" dialogue, in which characters literally state what's on their minds and how they feel. Most real people aren't that articulate except when they're in their therapist's office. They're also sufficiently socialized to adhere to the niceties of conversation (at least overtly).

Foreshadowing

A good script hints at what's to come, and dialogue is a useful tool for foreshadowing. In *Leap Year,* Aaron's "emergency labor whistle" is mentioned in the second scene of the first episode, while Aaron himself expresses concerns about his not having enough money for a hospital and being forced to have their baby in the woods. Both moments have a big payoff in the finale, when not only does Aaron use the emergency whistle but Lisa also ends up giving birth in the woods. Foreshadowing guides your viewer along your story's unfolding path, strengthens

LY EPISODE 10

https://vimeo.com/49768614

the structure and gives your audience the feeling that they're privy to something special. Then, when the foreshadowed elements come to pass, the payoff for those paying attention will help you win them over. This is especially true of an ongoing series. Give the viewers something to think about, suggest plot points and hook them, keep them wondering if what they *think* will happen actually *will*, get them on your fishing line and then reel 'em in.

LY EPISODE 10

Exposition and Backstory

The enemy of subtext is exposition. In fact, the arch nemesis of good scriptwriting is exposition. As soon as your characters start telling their entire life story, loudly explaining the theme of the script, or awkwardly telling everyone around them their emotional state, the script is doomed. Exposition is all telling, and as every writer, director or producer will constantly drill into your head—in film, you must always, always, always *show, not tell*.

Every character and every *world* has a past, and the backstory is that past. A lot of new writers make the mistake of having their characters explain their entire history in one, long monologue—avoid this like you'd avoid your face catching on fire. *You* should know every part of your world and characters' backstories, but as we discussed in Chapter 2, the audience should learn the important parts (the ones that relate directly to the central plot and theme of the show) slowly as the series unfolds.

IS IT A COMEDY OR A DRAMA?

There is a big difference between comedic dialogue and dramatic dialogue. One is *speed*. Many actors who have worked on comedies with Woody Allen have famously told the same story: he doesn't give many notes, but when he does, it's usually *"go faster."* Most comedy moves at lightning speed, like a high-energy symphony. When written well, the jokes work off of one another, each building on the last, not only providing new reasons to laugh but recapturing the previous ones. This is similar to the way you structure your story for rising action; the idea is to build the laughter until it peaks in a crescendo of hilarity. This is, as mentioned earlier, called *killing it,* and you want to do it in every comedic script you write.

Comedic dialogue must also be *specific.* It involves exact turns of phrase, precise spans of seconds in pauses and even specific numbers of words in sentences (brevity being the soul of wit). Yet (and here's the rub), the best comedic dialogue also sounds uncontrived, natural and realistic. Professional comedians refine their acts for hours upon hours; they polish and cut, they structure and build their jokes, and the result is a routine that feels like casual banter, but is in fact a tightly wrapped package with no joke missing its mark. The dialogue in a comedy is much the same.

On the other hand, dramatic dialogue is, well, dramatic. The rhythm and flow adjust to accommodate deeper or more complex themes. Drama is about emotion, about love, about death, and the characters take it all with a real-life, convincing seriousness. Dramatic dialogue tends to be slower, except in scenes of great urgency or emotional outburst. The kind of quips and jabs that comedies rely on are rarer in drama. When they do occur, they are there not so much for comedic "zing" as they are for providing momentary release from increasing tension between characters. Dialogue in a drama gives us a look into the heart of our characters, so philosophizing and monologizing are suitable for the form; they are an accepted and common part of the story world. In contrast, in comedy, long blocks of dialogue (especially those of the introspective, reflective sort) are often frowned upon.

Dramatic dialogue is not easy to write. It is really a study of human nature, experience and emotion, which if done without great care can come off feeling tired or cheesy. Comedic dialogue can be even harder to write, because it demands such a high level of specificity for razor sharp witticisms and observations, and because, well, you have to be *funny.*

COMEDIC DIALOGUE TECHNIQUES

The comedy writer has an arsenal of countless tools, but comedy is extremely hard, if not impossible, to teach. The key is to be honest with yourself and to ask yourself a very simple question: Are your scripts getting laughs? The only way to know if your comedy is working is to get feedback from a live audience, even if it's just one person. Workshopping (discussed in Chapter 5) is a great way to test the "punch" of your writing. If the response is flat, you know you have a lot of polishing to do. Ultimately, you want to cultivate an accurate assessment of your intuitive, natural style and taste. Perhaps you are, at heart, a dramatist. Even if you're not a funny writer, it doesn't mean you're not a *good* writer, and if comedy isn't your thing, don't despair—comedies almost never win Oscars. Even in the online video world, where comedy reigns, many shows take a more realistic or serious position with regard to the human experience. Examples include online series *Pioneer One* (http://www.pioneerone.tv/) and *Legion of Extraordinary Dancers* (http://thelxd.com/), both winners of 2012 Webby Awards.

That said, there *are* several useful and frequently used techniques and devices that will help you hone your comedic dialogue. Let's look at some of them.

The Call-Back Joke

The idea of the call-back is simple: bring back your jokes, episode by episode and even scene by scene. *Arrested Development* has dozens of call-back jokes—be it a terrible chicken dance attempted by every character, or asking, *"Her?"* every time someone falls in love with a strange or unattractive person. *Break a Leg* has similar jokes—from a cowboy riff heard every time *Swamblers* is mentioned (Episode 1 01:37, 01:57 and 04:16), to Chase Cougar's constant flow of accidental sexual

BaL EPISODE 1

https://vimeo.com/47527116

euphemisms. Though simple, the call-back joke can be a powerful tool. It rewards attentive fans, those who watch your series from the first minute to the last, and it makes them feel like they're a part of a special club; it can even turn a casual fan into a line-quoting machine (think of the fans of *Arrested Development, South Park, Monty Python's Flying Circus*, etc.).

Playing the Opposite

Have you ever had an entire conversation in which the main speaker describes something utterly terrible, and you respond as if you think the terrible thing is wonderful and amazing (or vice versa)? If you have, you were playing the opposite, probably to tease, ridicule or antagonize the main speaker. In *The Defenders of Stan,* Ted/Captain Ultra does this to Stan after Stan returns from his disappointing date. Seeing his brother slumped and defeated at home, Ted asks him with ironic feigned enthusiasm how his "big date" went. Stan is forced to endure the added humiliation of hearing from Ted how the date could have gone, and how Stan bitterly wishes it had gone. We know that Ted doesn't actually need information (or care about his brother's despair); he is using irony and sarcasm to hit the joke. When done with clever timing and a deadpan style, playing the opposite can provide a whole lot of laughs.

Double Entendre

A double entendre is a phrase with two meanings—the obvious one, and one that is often a bit more risqué. In the beginning of episode 2 of *Break a Leg* this exchange occurs:

DAVID

I never pegged you as a quitter.

AMBER

And you never *will* peg me, David.

DAVID

I don't think we're using peg in the same way.

In this exchange David's first sentence is very innocent, but *peg* has several meanings; one being *identify* and another you can probably figure out on your own.

The double entendre is a long-established comedy troupe. In *Romeo and Juliet,* the entire opening between Gregory and Samson is filled with double entendre. When Samson says, "Me they shall feel while I am able to stand," he isn't talking about being able to stand up on his legs. Shakespeare employs the double entendre quite often. Why? Because, no matter how civilized we are, how intelligent or educated, there's always room for a little bit of base humor—and when that base humor is wrapped in wit and subtlety, then you've got a very powerful and impressive package (see what we did there?).

Absurdism

The sketch troupe Monty Python was king of absurdist comedy. When absurdism's intended effect is to ridicule or point out the absurd in social convention or personal attitudes, it is firmly rooted in satire. For example, *Monty Python and the Holy Grail* is an utterly absurdist yet also pointed critique of medieval notions of chivalry, loyalty and the idealization of war. Satire is definitely not a requirement, though. Sometimes its purpose is simply high-end silliness, such as a man trying to return a dead parrot to a pet store. *Break a Leg* lives and breathes the absurd, residing somewhere between witticism and insanity—between "height disorders" (a not-so-subtle riff on weight disorders) and child actors who live in the sewers.

Mumblecore

Judd Apatow and his Hollywood crew popularized the mumblecore style of filmmaking. The heart of it is simple: make the dialogue as natural, off-the-cuff and conversational as possible. The comedy arises from genuinely believable moments that the audience has probably experienced themselves (or something close). These genuine moments are born of genuine-sounding dialogue, complete with stuttering, mumbling and all the other forms of natural, seemingly unscripted speech.

Though it has become ubiquitous in the last ten years or so, this form of dialogue is by no means new or revolutionary. Henrik Ibsen, author of the play *A Doll's House,* is considered by many to be the father of modern plays, because he moved away from the constructed, poetic expressions common in theater and instead used natural speech, including interruptions, misstatements and other quirks that would now be considered mumblecore. That said, Apatow and his actors wield it to near perfection, and it's become a prevalent comedic tool in recent films and TV shows.

COMEDIC AND DRAMATIC STYLES: WHAT'S YOURS?

Your style is an ever-evolving, ever-adapting creature. Along the way you will develop a writing voice, which will be heard loudly through the dialogue you write. Some writers create dialogue so distinctive that newer writers find themselves—willingly or not—imitating them. These masters have helped define our culture and our art, and there's nothing wrong with making their wisdom your own. Studying them closely will help you become a better writer. Here are four (though there are dozens more) whose names you have most likely heard and whose unique dialogue styles have shaped scriptwriting as we know it.

1. **William Shakespeare**: Shakespeare wrote dramatic and comedic dialogue with beauty and poetry. Shakespeare was so good with words he stopped using regular ones and started making up new ones. Shakespeare's dialogue truly is music, from the witty back-and-forth banter in his comedies to his famous dramatic monologues. It's no wonder that most scriptwriting rules come directly from his writing. That said, the Bard's dialogue is still poetry, and the world has, at least for now, moved away from iambic pentameter.

2. **Neil Simon**: Simon operates on natural, quick back-and-forth jabs with characters constantly fighting and arguing with one another. It's on the shoulders of Neil Simon and his contemporaries,

the great Woody Allen and Mel Brooks, that comedy as we know it stands.

3. **David Mamet**: Mamet's characters talk fast, cuss a lot and never finish a thought. They talk like . . . well, they never really . . . the one thing they *always do* is, well, they—it's their minds, you know? They're always changing them—usually mid-sentence. Mamet tries to emulate the way real people talk—if real people were all angry and had attention deficit disorder. His dialogue mimics real-life conversation. We interrupt each other and bounce from one subject to the other like drunken Ping-Pong balls. Mamet helped move theater and film away from its poetic, often stilted dialogue toward a more natural format.

4. **Aaron Sorkin**: Sorkin is like Mamet if Mamet cussed less and talked a thousand times faster. Sorkin's dialogue is built on speed, wit and intelligence (not that Mamet's isn't, but there's a rhythm to Sorkin that is unmistakable). If you look at a Sorkin script, you'll notice he breaks a big screenwriting rule; he's got a monologue on almost every page. He makes it work, however, with the sheer speed of his words. To get a Sorkin script to sound the way it should requires incredibly good actors capable of following his flow while maintaining extreme naturalism. It's hard, but when done well, the rhythm and music of his dialogue is near perfection. While there are faults in this style, shows like *The West Wing* are the very best TV has to offer.

As artists developing our own styles, we steal. We steal unwittingly, we steal on purpose, we steal because we're inspired and because stealing from masters is how we learn—and how our masters before us learned. Writers like those named above are just the tip of the iceberg, and to learn dialogue is to study the men and women who have excelled above all others in it.

Leap Year was heavily inspired by Sorkin. The writers wanted to squeeze 30 minutes of plot into their client's 8- to 9-minute length restriction. Furthermore, the characters were all smart and witty businesspeople who were great for showing the wit and intellect of the fast-talking Sorkin-style dialogue. The style remained the writers' own (especially the *Break a Leg*–esque humor), but the speed of the banter had a "Sorkinesque" quality that had an added bonus: Having a web show compared to the style of one of the best writers of our time gave it a credibility that few other things could. That said, it's important to not rip off the greats. There's a difference between being influenced by another writer and copying his or her work to such a degree that your script feels unoriginal and derivative. Every writer must walk that fine line.

Learn to feel the many different rhythms of dialogue, the different songs of different writers, and let them influence your own style until you become a unique mish-mash of the entire history of artistic genius.

CHAPTER 5

Revising and Polishing

You've followed your story outline, you've desperately tried to keep to your notes and you've finished the first draft of your script. The problem with a first draft is that as new ideas come up and you alter or replace what you've written, the story and characters also evolve. Story strands start coming loose, or perhaps you've focused so much on the story that the dialogue feels too informational. This is why the most common note after even the *best* first draft is, "It's not bad, it just needs to be punched up." You'll do this in two ways: first, just you and the script, alone, no distractions; then by sharing your script with readers and listeners who will give you spontaneous reactions and (hopefully) astute and useful feedback.

Throughout both of these ordeals, you need to be checking and honestly assessing three aspects of a successful script: the structure, the characters and the economy of your writing.

CHECKING YOUR STRUCTURE

Structure is the skeleton of your story. Because you're handling so many things in the generating phase of writing—so much to think about, so many decisions to make—structure often takes quite a beating in that first draft. So, as you reread, revise and polish your script, ask yourself whether each part of the script is doing its job.

Does the Setup Open with a Bang?

The first scene in any script is incredibly important, but even more so in a web series, because your audience is accustomed to giving online videos a quick glance before clicking away unless something immediately draws them in.

Does your first page (or minute) provide that hook? Does it kick off an intriguing, engaging story? Does it attract viewers to the characters and immerse them in the story world? Does it introduce the themes and the central question of the show? Does it give us a strong sense of the show's style? Have you put anything in that won't get resolved by the end? (You may have heard the rule of Chekhov's Gun: If you show a gun in the first act, it must be fired by the end of the story.) Do you see anything in your first few pages that are likely to end up as loose threads at the conclusion?

Does Act I Feel Like a Story?

After you've set up your story, the first act is the foundation for the rest of the script. Without it, the whole house topples. Ask yourself whether you have elaborated upon every problem introduced in the setup and planted the seeds of the B-story or C-story, if necessary. Ask yourself:

- Does every character continue to demonstrate his or her quirks, limitations and other personality traits?
- Does every character express his or her dramatic need or goal for that episode?

■ Have I used the dialogue and action to foreshadow the ongoing development of the characters and the complications/climax of the episode?

Does Act II Drive the Story Forward?

The second act is the journey, the heart of the story. This is where your characters deal with their problems and either defeat them or sink deeper into them. It needs to include two crucial plot points: the protagonist's failure to achieve his or her goal, and the one desperate, last-ditch effort to make everything work out (both internally and externally). The action should be leading us toward the ever-important second turning point and the stakes should be raised higher and higher. It also needs to connect to Act I. Ask yourself:

■ Am I developing every plot point that I introduced in Act I?

■ Is everything I mentioned in Act I—every seed of every plot point, joke or character trait that's relevant to the story—further developed in Act II?

■ Do the story and all of the characters' actions and motivations make sense thus far?

■ Does Act II lead the audience energetically and inevitably into the climax of Act III?

■ Most important: is it entertaining? (Ask yourself this question throughout the process.)

Does Act III Pay Off?

Act III is where everything comes together; it is the culmination of every plot point introduced in those first few pages, the climax of your entire episode. Act III needs to tie up every loose end. Check this by asking yourself:

■ Does it use every joke, every character trait, every wayward comment made throughout the script (preferably in Act I) to lead the characters to the climax and help them through it?

- Is it exciting?

- Does it end in a satisfactory way, with both the characters and the story staying consistent with the other acts?

- Is the conclusion—the last few pages—strong?

- Do the story and all of the characters' actions and motivations make sense?

- Does it make the audience want to watch the next episode once the credits roll?

When you can say "yes" to all of these questions, take a break to celebrate. The hardest part of editing is done. You've finished with the broad strokes of structure, and now you can get down to the more subtle tweaks and nitpicky adjustments that will really make your story glow.

CHECKING YOUR CHARACTERS

The two most important things to keep an eye out for as you're "punching up" your characters are whether they're consistent from beginning to end and whether they are suffering and responding to enough torment.

In a film, characters must change and grow over the course of their journey. In TV shows (especially sitcoms) and web shows, the rule is that characters' basic natures stay consistent across the entire series. This doesn't mean that your characters should never change one little bit, or that their relationships, jobs, etc. won't "trigger" them in different ways. But your characters' personalities, fundamental attitudes and problem-solving styles must remain the same. Otherwise your show loses its coherence, its identity, and probably its audience.

In *Dr. Horrible's Singalong Blog,* Dr. Horrible never really changes. Even though it might seem that he begins evil and ends good, his character isn't evil to start with; he is basically a good person on a misguided search for personal identity and potency in the world. The difficulties of living with such a dual nature play out across the entire series. His emotions deepen as he befriends Penny and competes with his rival for her affections. His professional ambitions evolve, but the seeds of his emotions were established quickly in the pilot and developed with consistency throughout the series.

In *Break a Leg,* the main character's basic nature does not change. David's ongoing situation produces some changes as we follow him from the beginning to the end of the series: he gains a bit more confidence, he starts letting the craziness of the other characters affect his own sanity a bit, and he gradually becomes a little more accepting of the loony world that he lives in. But the *essence* of the character never really changes: His dramatic need is consistent, as are his actions (doing everything he can to get his show made). His confidence might build and his tolerance for crazy may rise, but in the end he is still the same David we meet in the first episode.

In short, the thing to watch for when you're punching up is whether the character you introduce in the first scene of the first episode remains consistent—in dialogue and in action—in every situation he or she is thrust into.

CHECKING THE ECONOMY OF THE WRITING

In other words, *trim the fat.* The final step in punching up your script is to take a big, sharp knife and cut out anything unnecessary: dialogue that doesn't move the story or develop character; an orphaned plot point that never gets wrapped up; even full scenes that seemed pivotal in the early stages of writing but that you now must admit no longer work with the story. The reason that first drafts tend to be bloated is simple and perfectly forgivable: it is because in the generative phase, writers tend to overdo things. We want every nuance to be felt, every detail to stick in the viewers' minds, every character to be understood and loved (or hated). These are all wise and noble goals.

Here's the catch: Your audience probably needs less of what you're doing. You, as the writer, have to learn to give the viewers a bit of credit: trust in their imaginations, their willingness to suspend disbelief, their ability to respond to emotional fluctuations and their comprehension of plot and story arc. Do not beat the audience over the head with too much information, too much reinforcement of character or too much complexity of character or story. Today's audiences are constantly ready to click away and watch something else, so you want to avoid trying their patience with repetition and extraneous information. Your job is to grab that machete with both hands and go to town.

Of course, this ruthless assault on your script can feel agonizing, and making the drastic-but-necessary cuts can seem well-nigh impossible. But take heart: Scripts are *always* stronger after the writer cuts a few pages off the first draft. By clearing away the clutter, you create more room to rethink, to rewrite, to see what's really important and give it more weight.

Punching up a script is a long, exhilarating and maddening process. Very few writers can (or should) completely revamp a first draft all in one go. You might be a master of all-night writing frenzies, but revising takes time, no matter what. Deadlines are deadlines, so build in time to really read the script and consider every moment, every scene and every line of dialogue. Make sure the structure is ironclad and the story is compelling and strong, with every element doing its part. Be sure to take mental and physical breaks; go outside, play some sports, sing ecstatically into a hairbrush for a while. Otherwise, you'll exhaust yourself and start missing things you'll wish you'd caught.

When you're done with this solitary retreat with your script— yes, the *whole thing*—pat yourself on the back. Then brace yourself for Round Two: Script vs. Readers (that is, readers who aren't you).

GETTING FEEDBACK

Writing can be a lonely art. We toil in bedrooms and cafés, we write for hours and we play in our own worlds with no one to accompany us but our own strange characters. It's easy to fall in love with these quirky, fascinating people in our heads, the stories we build around them, and the words we use to tell those stories. By the time we have spent a month, six months, or more communing with our secret friends in their secret world, we become pretty sure that we know all there is to know and can write all that is necessary to write to bring all of it to life for an audience.

But there's a problem. It's called "the gap." This is the yawning chasm between the writer's mind and the viewer's perception. It contains all of the writer's unique life memories, attitudes and beliefs, aesthetic taste, and even subtler things like expectations of how cause and effect work, or the "logic" of emotions. As writers, we constantly project all of these things into our work, which is good because it gives the work voice and individuality—but it's also problematic because *the viewer doesn't share these projections*. Viewers have their own individual ideas about how the world works and why people are the way they are, based on their own life experiences.

Hence "the gap" between the writer and the viewer. Your job as a writer is to bridge that gap by listening to feedback that tells you what you have actually put on the page as opposed to what you think you put there.

Scriptwriters work in an audio-visual medium, which means that the words on the page read one way but sound another when spoken out loud or translated into a visual scene. What you hear and see in your mind is going to get filtered through a lot of other ears and eyes, and in that process you'll find that the plot point you thought you'd nailed is actually confusing to the audience, or that the joke you thought was the best part of the script falls flat.

So, again, writing is a lonely art—but bringing forth a finished script is a profoundly collaborative one. As happy as you've been spending quality time with your imaginary friends, and no matter how weird it might feel letting strangers come in and look around, it's the only way to move forward with the script. There are several ways to make this happen: the workshop, the staged reading, and the table reading.

The Workshop

The writer's workshop is a great way to get another writer's critical eye on your script. Your scriptwriting class might include workshops, or you can form or find a group of like-minded individuals and gather somewhere—preferably a place with a lot of coffee—and read one another's work as critically as possible, giving written and/or verbal notes, reflecting back to the writer what you see and hear as you read the script.

Many workshops are led by a professional (often a teacher or a writer) who knows story structure and is familiar with the most common difficulties encountered by new-ish writers. Even if you don't have access to such a facilitator, it's easy enough to find fellow writers in your classes and in the community. At the very least, a writer's group will push you to let someone besides yourself read the script and give you an honest response to it. Ideally, you'll have several talented readers who see the things you don't see and suggest small changes that help galvanize your script and transform it from good to great. Either way, the writing workshop is the first step to writing a good third (and fourth and fifth) draft.

A note on giving good workshop feedback: Saying you "like" something is not helpful. Saying you "don't like" something isn't helpful, either. "Like" isn't a word that should come up in a workshop. In fact, aesthetic taste should be checked at the door. Your job as a workshop partner is to read closely and *analytically* and apply what you know about story structure, character development, etc. You don't want to make anyone feel bad, and no one wants to make you feel bad, either; but you won't be helping each other if you don't dig in and do the work.

The Staged Reading

A staged reading is exactly what it sounds like. You appoint your classmates, or enlist actors (the most capable ones you can find), and have them act out your show in front of the class or on a stage in front of an audience who will share their thoughts on the script afterward. Regardless of what you manage to put together and where and with whom, the reading is a necessary part of the editing process. Getting input from other writers in a workshop is great, but they're still not *hearing* and *seeing* the story, which means many flaws won't be apparent. The live performance can make all the difference.

An important aspect to the reading is to get good actors and to have a few rehearsals with them before doing the reading in front of the audience. It doesn't necessarily matter whether the actors at the table reading are the actors who will eventually play the roles (though that would be ideal). However, it is important that the actors are skilled. Hearing the story is essential; if the actors don't do the dialogue justice, they can make the script sound bad and create flaws that wouldn't be there if you had a better group of actors. Talk to them, work with them, get them to refine the timing and the voices of the characters. Then, when you're ready, get them in front of an audience and see the magic happen.

A staged reading might not involve performing all of the stage directions fully (especially when they call for fighting, sex, car chases, etc.), but it's helpful if the performers can work in some gesture and movement to help the audience better envision your story.

The reading should end with a talk-back in which the audience tells you what they thought of the whole thing. Take notes, listen and don't get defensive. Even if the response is lukewarm or even negative, it's better to hear it *now* instead of *later,* when you've already invested a tremendous amount of time and energy into refining (and maybe even producing) the episodes.

A reading is especially important for web series because it not only helps you craft a strong story (something that is sorely lacking in the online-entertainment space), but it also lets you witness a live audience response, something you can't get from posting your video on YouTube.

The Table Reading

You've written and rewritten, you've heard it, you've seen it, you've gotten a ton of wanted and unwanted criticism, and now it's finished. You've cast it and are ready to shoot. Right? *Almost.* The final step of making your script pretty is the table read, where you, the director, possibly a producer or two, and the entire cast sit down and read your script out loud.

The table reading is not just another staged reading. In a table reading, the people who are actually going to bring the script to life are the ones you get to see and hear, and you will find that some tweaking here and there is desirable. In fact, you should expect your final script to change fairly significantly during the table reading—not its structure, but its nuances and finer points, especially in dialogue. No matter how good the actors (or classmates) for your initial reading were, you now have an official and probably different cast. Actors have different ways of talking, interpreting scenes, delivering lines and displaying emotions. As a result, the lines you thought worked before may not work now. Furthermore, you may get ideas for moments that work *specifically* with one of your actors that wouldn't have been possible before you had the final cast. And the actors themselves will nearly always offer variations, riffs and ad-libbed dialogue that make you cry, "Someone write that down!"

The table reading also gives the director, cinematographer, and other key crew members a chance to visualize and get a feel for your story. If artistic differences are going to emerge, it's good to talk about them before you're on location. It's also better for the director and others to ask questions and for you to think through possible answers now rather than on-set, when time is a precious commodity. A lot can happen during the table reading: An actor may have a different idea about how to play a character; the director may want to change a location or a motivation; one or more parties may be confused about a line of dialogue or a plot point. The sooner you can deal with these issues, the better.

Sifting Through the Critiques

Once your script is finished, it stops being your baby and joins a much bigger family. The actors and crew will bring their own thoughts, quirks and individual flavor to your writing. Thus, it is important to know how to take feedback—when to listen, when to ask more questions, when to oblige and even when to be a "difficult" writer. The world will often see fit to give you its opinion, whether you want it or not. As a writer, your job is to know when to listen and when to fight.

Sometimes, the problem is obvious. Sometimes, a note will just feel *right*. Other times, you'll notice a criticism will keep popping up no matter who you give the script to. A good rule of thumb is if more than three or four people mention it, it's definitely a problem.

You'll also get contradictory notes. In these situations ask yourself, "Who are the note-givers?" If you trust the reader or he or she is a director you chose to help you with your series or a producer who is running the show, then it's in your best interest to hear them out. On the other hand, some people like to comment on everything. You know those friends, the ones who will loudly explain why every film isn't good enough. They may not be trustworthy, and for whatever reason they may be unable to plainly say, *I like it*.

Working with Bosses

Higher-caliber web series often have a brand or a network attached; when you've got money, you've got bosses. The bosses all have their own jobs to do and their own agendas; maintaining the integrity of the story is not often one of them. You have to be diplomatic here. No one is going to work with an unreasonable writer, so learn to pick your battles. Sometimes a calm, logical explanation of why a suggestion doesn't work will be enough to convince the suggester to drop it. Brands (or rather, the people in charge of articulating and managing brand identity) are infamous for ruining good series, but then again, as an artist, you must be able to work within requirements and restrictions. If a brand kills one idea, you should have 15 more ideas ready to fire. It's a two-way street, and a good web show writer also needs a good head for business. You, the writer, want to tell a story; your client wants to make money; and somewhere in the middle is a compromise that creates a strong series and pleases everyone—*The Guild* (www.watchtheguild.com/), *The Bannen Way* (www.crackle.com/c/The_Bannen_Way/), and *Leap Year* are great examples of how this can actually work out to everyone's satisfaction.

All in all, most web series are not brand-sponsored. This means that the writer will have complete creative control. Be careful! If you have full control, it's even more important that you seek and carefully consider reader/audience feedback. Passion is good, but passion plus ignorance will only hurt your script.

A good artist listens to everyone—perhaps without agreeing, perhaps without changing a thing. But he or she does listen, think, observe, analyze and toil over every tiny detail of his or her work. This is what it takes to turn an idea into a great story.

CHAPTER 6

Episode 2 and Beyond

We've talked about structure when it comes to a single episode of a series, but what about the whole season? After all, part of the appeal of a series is the fact that we can follow our favorite characters as they go through their lives, face challenges and ultimately change and evolve. Just as a single episode has a story arc that becomes a framework to tell a particular story, so should a season have a structure that shapes the individual episodes into a larger framework. This is the series arc. When planned right, this order ensures that the characters evolve consistently and that each episode leads us to a climactic season finale that provides both a resolution and an intriguing setup for the following season.

SERIALIZED VS. STANDALONE

Although it might seem obvious to you why you're writing a series and not, say, a movie, you should ask yourself some logistical questions so you can structure your season(s):

- What am I trying to achieve by telling the story using short episodes?

- What links those episodes together?

Do you want to use your characters to tell a series of standalone stories? Or do you want to tell a more complex story that requires multiple episodes or even seasons? (Another way to think of this is writing a collection of short stories vs. writing a novel divided into chapters.) The answers to these questions will largely dictate how you structure your show.

The Standalone Approach

Let's consider a series with standalone episodes. This type of series features a cast of characters who in every episode find themselves in a new, never-before-encountered situation (though one that perpetuates the basic premise and themes of the show). They are faced with a problem, baffled by the problem, solve (or don't solve) the problem and never speak of it again. A viewer can miss an episode or two and still understand pretty much everything that's happening when he or she next tunes in. Standalone episodes rarely refer to previous episodes, and when they do the reference is not critical to understanding the plot of the current episode. One example is *Elevator Stories* (http://ny.channel101.com/show.php?show=272), a series of vignettes captured on an elevator security camera. The characters (who, incidentally, are sock puppets) aren't particularly developed as individuals, and the vignettes are mostly independent of each other. Another is *Yacht Rock* (www.channel101.com/show/171), which tells the "story of smooth music." Each episode features a fictional drama surrounding the creation of a particular song, and again the episodes are independent of each other. In both cases, a framework holds the series together, but the episodes could be viewed in any order and it wouldn't matter if a viewer missed some.

Sitcoms, both on TV and online, function in a similarly stand-alone mode. Each episode introduces a crisis situation that is resolved by the end. While some of the show's story arcs may keep evolving (romantic relationships, etc.), the characters themselves do not change. Even if a viewer was to miss half a season, he or she would return to find the same characters acting in the same familiar way week after week.

One advantage of the standalone episode is that the viewer does not have to commit to watching the show every single week to stay up to date with the story. On the other hand, the standalone format is less conducive to building complex characters or telling intricate stories that span many episodes. Change does happen over time in these shows, but in minute (and sometimes only vaguely sig-nificant) increments. This avoids confusing (and hence losing) less frequent viewers.

The Serialized Approach

In contrast, a serialized show is highly dependent on continuity from episode to episode. Should a viewer miss an episode of this type of show, or tune in halfway through a season, she may feel lost as char-acters discuss situations or face problems that were introduced in earlier episodes. Or worse, those episodes are *not* referred to, so the viewer is even more lost. The web is highly conducive to serialized storytelling. Web shows enjoy a certain freedom from the danger of missing episodes because in most cases, every episode is free and eas-ily available, often in a single location such as the show's website or a YouTube playlist. If a viewer stumbles across episode 2 or 10 or 15 of a show, he can pause to catch up on the previous episodes. Or he could watch the pilot and come back six months later to watch episode 2. Some web series, such as *The Guild* and *Dr. Horrible's Singalong Blog*, are available on DVD and streaming services such as Netflix. What-ever the means of distribution, it's crucial that serialized shows offer the audience a chance to catch up on missed episodes. This allows writers to widen the scope of their stories and increase the complexity of their characters, knowing that they aren't limited to providing "snack-sized" standalone videos.

Let's take the highly serialized web series *Break a Leg* as an example. Each episode of the series has its own three-act structure in which the characters are confronted with a problem, experience conflict and finally solve the problem. However, the first season of the series quickly departs from the location and story established in the first few episodes. A viewer who watches the pilot episode, in which David Penn becomes a writer on a show with no budget, and then watches episode 5, in which David and the gang travel through a surreal landscape of haunted hotels and warring child actors to fulfill a prophecy, will be hopelessly confused. Each episode of *Break a Leg* assumes that the viewer has seen all previous episodes and understands what's happening at each point in the season's story arc. If the viewer hasn't seen every episode, he or she will miss most of the significant story and character developments and process only the bare plot structure of that episode.

One of the main goals of *Break a Leg* is to immerse the viewer in the evolving mythology of the series' fictional Hollywood. Missing episodes of the show would detract from this experience, so the creators "require" the viewer to have seen all episodes in order. This freed the writers to draw upon story elements from earlier episodes and use what they had already established to enrich the plots, character motivations and themes of later episodes—a very economical as well as effective technique. This also allowed the writers to explore the long-term effects of each incident upon the characters. By spreading the story out over the course of many episodes, the serialized show can attain more intricacy and more in-depth characters.

Such series often attract die-hard fans who watch every episode and almost feel like they have a personal relationship with the characters. The downside is that the show's world can often seem inaccessible to new viewers. One way to alleviate this problem is by building in other forms of continuity.

Recurring Themes and Characters

One way to add continuity to a show is to introduce recurring themes and/or characters. This approach can benefit both serialized and standalone shows. The idea is that you introduce a story or character element and then let it resolve or "disappear" in that episode, then return to it later in the season or in a future season. In the case of a standalone show, infrequent viewers might not recognize the element or character, but because the main characters are familiar and the episode story arc follows the expected pattern, they will not be thrown. At the same time, the dedicated viewer will be rewarded with "inside" knowledge.

An example of this approach is *The X-Files*. The writers found an interesting way to cater to die-hard fans without alienating new viewers. Most episodes of the show were standalones in that agents Mulder and Scully encountered and solved some sort of a supernatural mystery or crime. In addition, each season included several episodes dedicated to "the conspiracy" that Mulder is sworn to expose. Mulder believes that this conspiracy was responsible for the disappearance of his sister; in each conspiracy episode, he moves closer to the resolution of that intermittently appearing plotline.

The conspiracy episodes of *The X-Files* were highly serialized and featured recurring characters (the cigarette-smoking man, Spender) as well as recurring themes (alien abductions and implants). *The X-Files'* characters and themes made the conspiracy episodes incomprehensible to less frequent viewers. However, because those episodes were fairly rare, the casual viewer only had to endure one hour of confusion before returning the next week for a satisfying episode of the familiar standalone format.

Regardless of whether a show is standalone or serialized, it's good practice to build in some form of continuity. Recurring themes and characters add depth to the story and the opportunity to develop and change them in ways that can't be done in a series with strictly standalone episodes.

THREE-ACT STRUCTURE FOR A SERIALIZED SHOW

We've discussed the three-act structure as it applies to an individual episode of a series, but this structure can be applied to a whole season as well. Think about a show's season as just another story that's told over the course of many episodes. Of course, the more serialized the show, the more relevant the three-act structure. For instance, a season of *Star Trek* does not need a strong three-act structure connecting the episodes (missions). On the other hand, a show like the web series *Leap Year* benefits greatly from it.

Before we discuss how the three-act structure applies to a whole season, let's review what it is. The *setup* introduces the problem that will drive the plot, establishes the characters and their motivations and raises the central question. *Rising action* depicts the characters' struggle with the problem as the stakes are raised and the obstacles increase, their failed attempts to solve the problem, and the sudden reversal of their fortunes. At that point, the *resolution* presents that do-or-die moment that answers the episode's central question. Now let's see how this applies to a serialized show with a well-defined season arc.

The Setup

Just as the setup of an episode is its first minute or few minutes, the setup act of a season is usually the first few episodes. The characters are introduced and their motivations made clear. The season's central question is posed, and the characters find themselves at a crossroads—the season takes a turn in a new direction. Each episode in this setup phase will have its own plot, its own central question and so on, but it will also serve the larger purposes of the season's arc.

In *Leap Year,* the first three episodes comprise the setup act. The characters are introduced in the pilot, and we learn that there is danger on the horizon as the characters are in fear of losing their jobs. Episode 2 confirms those fears when all of them are in fact fired. In episode 3, as the friends rent an office, decide to start their own companies and learn about the business contest sponsored by a mysterious investor, the central question of the series is posed: "Will these characters succeed at being entrepreneurs?"

Note that *Leap Year* is a highly serialized show. If you begin watching at episode 3, you may have some idea of who the characters are and you will likely be able to mostly follow the plot, but you will miss the emotional and psychological depth that developed in episodes 1 and 2. The characters' basic identities and life situations are established (Aaron has a family and a child on the way; Derek is a bit of a screw-up; Jack seems to want to get fired). This knowledge increases our investment in the characters and heightens the tension as they encounter each crisis; it intensifies our need for an answer to the central question.

Rising Action

The rising action portion of the season (Act II) consists of episodes that build toward a dramatic turning point, which in turn sets up the climax. The stories in these episodes increase the pressure on the main characters in the context of the central question. Ideally, by the end of this portion of the season, the viewer should expect the opposite of what will actually happen in the resolution. For instance, if the central question is whether the characters will succeed at something, we want the viewer to think that they can't possibly, no way, not after everything that has happened. You, the writer, want it to seem less and less likely that success is possible until the *reversal of fortunes,* or the season's second turning point.

Leap Year's Act II consists of episodes 4 through 8. Throughout these episodes the characters experience the triumphs and setbacks of running their own companies—with the emphasis on the setbacks. Each episode contributes to the characters' growing desperation to do something in the face of mounting pressure. For example, throughout Act II Aaron spends more and more time at work, but the jobs he's doing—helping his brother, explaining financial concepts for free to customers whose work has already been done—aren't yielding the financial payoff he needs (for the reasons established in the setup: his wife's pregnancy, his fears of failing). On top of that, he's exhausted and starting to make mistakes that further endanger his already faltering business. Finally, in episode 5, Jack and Olivia betray Aaron, psychologically and emotionally pushing him over the edge. The other characters have all hit rock bottom as well, and by the end of the episode, the friends can't even seem to tolerate each other, much less get their businesses running. Effectively, they've given up. The troubles, both personal and professional, have been piling up until this turning point. This is the moment when *something has to change:* the characters' fortunes must be reversed somehow.

The change comes via Bryn's idea to merge all of the characters' companies into one business focused on her videoconferencing idea.

LY EPISODE 8

https://vimeo.com/49172836

She recruits Jack to help her and he, in turn, makes amends with Aaron, Olivia and Derek. Voila! By the end of episode 8, the friends are friends again (mostly), they have a new business plan and their prospects don't seem as grim. Note that the reversal of fortune pertains directly to the central question: "Will the friends succeed at being entrepreneurs?" At the beginning of this episode the answer is leaning heavily toward "no." But by the end, we're starting to think that maybe, just maybe—"Yes!"

Resolution

After the reversal of fortunes (Act II, second turning point) and the characters' regrouping for a final shot at achieving their goal, the remaining episodes should build rapidly to the season's climax and denouement, which answer the season's central question and hook the viewer to watch the following season.

Leap Year's resolution takes place over the course of episodes 9 and 10. The friends determine that they need two things to finish their demo in time to present it to the investor: the help of a reclusive engineer as well as money to pay him for his help. In episode 9, Aaron and Olivia secure the funding, and in episode 10 the friends embark on an adventure to find the engineer.

Episode 10 is the climax of the season. All season-long plotlines are tied together, all major conflicts are resolved and the central question is answered. We learn that the mysterious benefactor is Andy Corvell, the friends' eccentric former boss, who fired them and set them on the path of entrepreneurship as a business lesson for his remaining employees. We learn that Bryn has been spying for Andy (hinted at in episode 6) and that Derek was the one who stole the communal server (the return of which enables the friends

LY EPISODE 10

https://vimeo.com/49768614

to complete the crucial demo). Lisa gives birth (captured live on camera during a videoconference); her "performance" impresses Andy and ultimately leads to the five friends sharing the $500,000 prize.

It's not mandatory that every single plotline be resolved at the end of the season; for example, *Leap Year* leaves Derek's sexual harassment lawsuit unresolved, to be continued in the following season. But as a rule, the season will feel stronger and tighter if you can unite *most* of your threads into one clear whole. The purpose of the three-act structure—in a season as well as an episode—is to hook the viewer into following your story every step of the way toward a satisfying conclusion. The more you (surprisingly) resolve in your climax and the more (cleverly) you tie the seemingly separate stories of your season together, the more satisfying the payoff at the end.

Looking Ahead

Leap Year gives the viewer a hint of what's to come in season 2. The friends meet with Andy at the end of episode 10 and are presented with three clear options: they can come back to their old jobs, they can take the money and see where their new company goes or they can sue Andy for wrongful termination. In addition, we know that Derek will have to face his sexual harassment lawsuit. This type of foreshadowing is extremely important for a series as you'll want to maintain the delicate balance between providing a satisfactory resolution to the current season and intriguing the viewer with the question, "What happens next?"

This question can be asked in a variety of ways. In *Leap Year*, the season's main plot is fully resolved, but the creators let the viewer know that this resolution has consequences that will be key

LY EPISODE 10

to the plot of the following season. Another approach might be to throw a catastrophe at the characters in the season finale. This has the effect of making the next season "must-see"—but it can also alienate viewers who may feel like they've invested time and attention only to be strung along until the next season to find out what happens next. The key to success with the latter method is to make sure that there is a clear resolution to the current season's story arc before the characters get thrown under the bus again (or rather, under a whole new bus).

SECONDARY STORY ARCS

We've discussed the three-act structure as it applies to a story told over the course of a season. All of the episodes in the season contribute something to this arc, and the story is brought to a satisfactory resolution at the end. This is not the *only* story told during the season, however. To really bring your show to life, the characters must go through a variety of experiences that change them. It would be awfully boring if your characters always stayed the same, so make sure that all characters (or at least all of the main characters) develop in new ways over the course of a season. Secondary story arcs are a great tool for bringing about character change, and for tying the whole plot together into a coherent whole.

There are several secondary story arcs in *Leap Year,* each featuring its own smaller-scale three-act structure. Let's take Lisa's pregnancy as an example. We learn early in the season that Lisa is pregnant and this fact weighs heavily on Aaron's mind. This is our setup. As Aaron's business interferes more and more with his personal life, we get to Aaron's worst nightmare, his "rock bottom": Lisa goes into labor in the woods. (This nightmare scenario is actually posited as a joke in the first episode, serving as a reoccurring theme.) The reversal of fortunes comes when Lisa has the idea to capitalize on the situation and deliver the baby on camera in a videoconference to impress Andy. This is our rising action. Finally, the arc is resolved when Lisa has the baby and Andy is impressed enough to give the friends the prize money.

In this example the arc focuses on a supporting character's role in shaping the life of the main character. Aaron's reactions to Lisa's pregnancy and his treatment of Lisa throughout help develop Aaron's character. It motivates Aaron, but otherwise doesn't affect the plot—until the very end when Lisa suddenly becomes instrumental in the resolution. Not all secondary arcs will (or should) play such a significant part in the resolution. It is, however, good form to use at least some of the secondary arcs to help resolve the main arc. These types of resolutions have a much more "polished" feel and instill a kind of confidence in the viewer that *nothing happened without a reason.* All of the different plotlines in a show become pieces of a puzzle and the viewer is delighted when all of the pieces are put together in the end.

Format

The first thing experienced screenplay readers and editors notice when reading a script is the format, which quickly and without fail tells if the writer is (a) good, (b) experienced and (c) dedicated to his or her craft. It's extraordinarily rare to come across a script where the content is good but the formatting is not.

A poorly formatted script implies that the writer didn't bother to learn the rules of the trade before diving into it. It suggests that a certain level of professionalism is lacking and that the script is the work of an amateur. In short, it's like showing up to your first business meeting in shorts and flip-flops: It ruins the entire presentation.

If we haven't driven the point home yet, I'll add that in the world of web shows, where budgets are hard to come by and credibility even harder, you always want to put your best foot forward.

The first thing that most people see in a new project is the script—that's how you'll hire the best actors and the best crew willing to give it their all for very little. If you want people to put countless hours into helping you realize your script, you have to put in a few of your own hours making sure the script looks as good as possible.

This chapter is a simple guide to proper screenplay formatting. Note that many writers have their own variations that they tend to stick to and many shows and production companies have house styles; each script formatting software will have slight variations as well. However, all script formatting is built on the idea of delivering necessary information efficiently and clearly. If you understand the logic behind the formatting, you'll be good to go.

When you look at a script, you'll see three major elements: the heading (or slugline), the action (or scene description) and dialogue. We will discuss formatting guidelines for each of these. And if you want to jump ahead and see a sample script, one is provided in the appendix.

HEADINGS

*T*raditionally, scripts start with the words FADE IN (or FADE UP, or TITLE UP), depending on what we see first. If your first shot is a sweeping shot of a vast landscape, then SLOW FADE IN works well. If your opening shot starts right in the action, a fade isn't necessary or appropriate; just start with your first *slugline*. A slugline tells the reader (and, most importantly, the pre-production and production crew) three things:

1. Whether the scene is shot inside (INT.) or outside (EXT.). Every scene starts with this information, no exceptions.

2. Where the scene is shot (location).

3. Whether the scene is DAY or NIGHT.

Sluglines are formatted like this:

INT. HOUSE – LIVING ROOM – NIGHT

Note that this example includes "INT." because the scene takes place inside a house. Whether a shot is interior or exterior depends on where the camera is. For instance, if you have a shot that shows characters in a car, are we (the viewers) "in the car" with the characters, or do we see the outside of the car? If we see the outside of the car, the camera is outside, so the slugline must say EXT. If the camera is really close to the car and pointing straight into the window, but we can still see the outside of the car, we are still EXT. However, if all we see is the inside of the car—as if we are in it too—the slugline would read INT.

Next comes the location, which is often broken up into two parts as shown above. The first part is the basic location, which can be general (a house, an office, a park) or more specific (Bob's house, Widget Corp. office, Central Park). If there are several "sub-locations" that are part of this basic location, these are indicated following a dash:

INT. HOUSE – BEDROOM – DAY

EXT. SAN FRANCISCO – LOMBARD STREET – NIGHT

INT. CAR – BACKSEAT – DAY

The entire slugline is always capitalized. Some writers (often TV writers) also underline. This lets the entire production team easily find every scene to be shot in a particular location, so those sets can be dressed, lit, etc. for several scenes to be shot together, rather than setting them up again and again. This is why it is extremely important to always indicate locations the same way. For instance, you would never write INT. BOB'S HOUSE – CLOSET – DAY in one scene and later write INT. BOB'S PENTHOUSE SUITE – WALK-IN CLOSET – DAY. That would cause the production team to think there were two locations they needed to use, when really there is only one.

Finally, the elements DAY and NIGHT give crucial information as well. They tell the production team that they will need to use a location both during the day and at night (this is important for sched-uling, permits, etc.), and they also let the lighting crew know that within a particular location they will need to prepare for both. The set dressers might also need to know so they can make an apartment look like it's morning and someone has just left, or like it's evening and someone has just come home.

Sometimes in scripts you will see more specific time elements giv-en, such as DAWN or DUSK. Be careful of these. It's easy for a writer to trick himself into thinking he has communicated something, when in fact only the people who see the slugline will ever know. For instance, if the writer puts INT. BOB'S BEDROOM – 6:30 A.M., how is the audi-ence going to know what time it's supposed to be? They never see the slugline. The writer needs to put the "6:30 a.m." information in the scene description following the slugline, perhaps via a clock showing the time, so that the audience will get the information.

There is one thing you must never, ever do in a slugline, and that is add information beyond INT./EXT., location and day/night. There must be no action, no dialogue, no scene description—noth-ing but the three basic elements. Here are some examples of what not to do in a slugline:

- INT. RESTAURANT – WAITRESS SERVING COFFEE – DAY. Clearly, "waitress serving coffee" is not a location; it belongs in the next element we'll discuss, the scene description (action).

- EXT. CENTRAL PARK – JOGGERS – DAY. Again, "joggers" are not a location. You could write "JOGGING PATH" instead, and in the action indicate that people are jogging.

- EXT. BASEBALL GAME – CHEERING CROWD – DAY. This one almost makes sense, but there are a few problems. A "game" is not a location; a "stadium" is, or a "high school baseball diamond." Likewise, a "cheering crowd" is not a location, but you could say "bleachers" or "stands." If you write "cheering crowd" as the location, does that mean that the camera is down on the field pointing up into the crowd? Or does it mean the camera is sitting next to someone in the bleachers? Remember, your sluglines do a job: they tell everyone on the production team exactly what they need to do, and where. Your locations need to be actual places; everything else is what we see in the scene, so save it for the action section of your script.

ACTION

Your action, or scene description, contains all of the information except dialogue that the actors, the director and anyone who is helping set up the location needs. Your first job as a writer is to communicate this information clearly and efficiently. Writers have different styles of presenting this information, but you should know about useful formatting conventions that can help keep your script's action readable and clear. The main two are capitalization and camera directions.

Capitalization

When a character *first* appears in a script, capitalize his or her name. After that first appearance, stop capitalizing the name.

Often, writers will capitalize specific actions or objects that are important to the story. This can function as a way to remind the production team that this moment or object is essential to the logic and clarity of the scene and it's not something that a director can omit or replace.

An example:

INT. BASEMENT – NIGHT

DAVID PENN is TIED to a chair. He has a BLACK EYE and generally looks haggard. The tip of a GUN is pressed firmly against his head.

BaL EPISODE 1

https://vimeo.com/47527116

The capitalization here sets necessary details apart from the *stage business* (gestures, movements, props, etc.) that gives the reader a more visual sense of the scene but that could be adjusted by the actors, set dressers, director, etc. For instance, the previous scene could have been written like this:

> INT. BASEMENT – NIGHT
>
> DAVID PENN is TIED to a broken office chair. He has a BLACK EYE and generally looks haggard, maybe hung over, maybe sleep-deprived. The tip of a GUN is pressed firmly against his head. He is chewing gum and repeatedly licks his lips in nervousness.

There is a lot of stage business in this version: the speculation about why he looks haggard, the gum, the lip-licking. This is detail that helps the reader's visual imagination, and that might inspire the cast and crew to have some creative ideas for a great-looking scene. The use of capitalization helps the reader's eye land immediately on the nonnegotiable elements, which is a big plus when production is under way and everyone needs to work accurately and efficiently.

You can also capitalize important sounds if they are not typical of the location or scene. For instance, if your main character's apartment is located next to a construction site, then construction sounds are going to be normal for that location. If they are mentioned at all they probably won't be capitalized. But let's say you have a scene in that location where a foghorn is heard. When you write your scene description, include a sentence like this: "A FOGHORN sounds amid the usual construction noises." The word *foghorn* is capitalized because it is necessary to the scene and a special sound the post-production team needs to notice.

These capitalization guidelines are partly a matter of style. Some professional scripts don't do it at all, while others do it to almost every new element introduced. It's the writer's decision whether and how much to use it.

Camera Directions

This formatting convention is easy. Never, ever write camera directions. No tilting, panning, zooming in—nothing that would involve actually touching the camera. Everyone on the production team has a job to do, and it's important to respect each member's expertise. You are the writer; the director is the director. Would you want the director hovering over you and telling you what the characters should say next? Then you shouldn't tell the director where to put the camera. Your job is to set the scene; he or she will figure out when to pan.

You are allowed, at times and with great restraint, to indicate certain perspectives within a scene. For instance, if your scene is set in a sports bar that has a TV on the wall, and you want to let the audience see what's on the TV, you can use an "ANGLE ON." It looks like this:

INT. SPORTS BAR – NIGHT

A rowdy crowd of Giants fans drink and cheer as they follow the game on the bar's TV. Suddenly, the bartender gestures for quiet and raises the TV volume. Everyone stares at the TV.

ANGLE ON: TV

A young female reporter stands on Ocean Beach, in front of an oncoming tidal wave.

ANGLE ON: BARTENDER

The bartender reaches for a framed picture above the cash register; it's the same young female reporter. He starts to cry.

Another type of scene you might occasionally indulge in is the POV, or point-of-view shot. For instance, you might have a scene witnessed by someone looking through binoculars. Or you might switch to the perspective of a small child whose eyeline is at knee level to the adults. You can indicate these shots as:

POV: SMALL CHILD

The small child wanders through the crowd of knees, occasionally peeking up a skirt.

If this point of view is necessary to the story—perhaps the child glimpses a gun strapped to a leg under one of those skirts, and the audience needs to see the gun (not just hear the child say that he or she saw a gun)—then use it.

Writers are allowed to do this kind of thing only when it would be clunky and confusing to explain all of that action in prose, or because a certain visual really is nonnegotiable to the story. However, don't go overboard and write your whole script divided into camera shots; you'll annoy everyone on the production team.

These conventions might seem like common sense, but it's surprising how many writers are tempted to intrude on the director's job. Scriptwriters tend to be visual thinkers who naturally want to transcribe exactly what they imagine onto the page. It's easy to get attached to that personal vision and to feel like it has to be exactly that way or it won't work. But every production is a collaborative effort, and many visions are being actualized—those of the writer(s), the actors, the director, the music composers, the editors. You, as the writer, get to go first: You give everyone else the blueprint to work with. But beyond that, much will be out of your hands. So your best strategy is to write your script with strong story logic, emotional focus and clarity, so the people in charge of taking it from the page to the screen will be inspired by your vision and make their aesthetic choices accordingly.

Style

There are various styles for writing action. Some writers invest a lot of time (and page space) in crafting vivid, poetic or blow-by-blow descriptions. Others provide the minimal information required for the reader and/or director to get what they need to understand the scene.

Compare these scene descriptions:

Looking wildly about him, Bob spots a vicious-looking rat. He gags, struggles to collect his wits and draws his gun.

Bob sees rat, draws gun.

The first provides a good deal of mood and visual detail. In contrast, the second sticks to the necessary facts. Neither of these styles is necessarily better than the other. Both provide the essential information the actors and director need. The longer one helps everyone "sink in" to the mood and feel of the scene. The potential problem with the longer one, though, is that you might end up with such wordy scene descriptions that the reader will have to skim for the necessary information.

Another danger is that there will simply be too many lines of action on the page. Most scripts with single-spaced dialogue should time out to about a page per minute. This is important when, for instance, a two-page scene gets cut. How will the production team know whether they just lost 30 seconds or four minutes? This is why simple, clear scene descriptions are generally best. They don't have to be sterile or bare-bones, but they should be free of distracting or overwhelming verbiage.

Keeping your style "clean"

In scriptwriting, every word either helps by giving necessary information or hurts by cluttering up the page. How do you know what's clutter and what's necessary? Here are a few common forms of clutter that are easy to check for:

1. *Adjectives:* If you're describing a character's "long, curved, cherry-red-painted clawlike false fingernails," that's clutter. And, unless every single one of those details is "nonnegotiable," you're intruding on the make-up and wardrobe department's job. Instead, give only as much description as it takes to communicate a basic idea of the character: maybe she has "sharp fake nails" or "cherry red nails" or "nails like claws." Or maybe you don't need any of that information to characterize this person, in which case leave it out.

2. *Adverbs:* If you write, "Bob slowly turns carefully and deliberately, drawing his gun silently and grimly," you've got clutter. And you're directing the actor, which is not your job. Stick to the basic movements needed for the scene: "Bob turns and draws his gun." The adverb *quickly,* by the way, is almost always unnecessary. "He quickly runs." "He quickly ducks." "She quickly hides the gun behind her back." Is there a non-quick way to do these things? Not really. Forget you ever heard that word. (Also be careful with *suddenly, immediately* and *totally.* Use these only if you're sure it wouldn't be obvious anyway.)

3. *Repetition:* "Bob turns. As he turns, he draws his gun. With his gun drawn, he shoots." Why repeat every action after it has

already been established? This should read: "Bob turns, draws his gun and shoots."

4. *Other unnecessary words:* In conversation, we often say things that don't belong in a well-crafted, uncluttered script. Here are a few that happen all the time:

- "Bob walks over to the fridge." The word *over* contributes nothing to the sentence, so it's clutter. Lose it: "Bob walks to the fridge." See how omitting one word keeps the line clean?

- "Bob starts to go to the door." Or: "Sally starts to pour the tea." Why is the phrase "starts to" there? What are we seeing, exactly? Do we see Bob go to the door? Do we see Sally pour the tea? If so, then "starts to" is clutter. However, if Bob is stopped in his tracks and doesn't make it to the door, or if Sally drops dead before she can actually pour the tea, then "starting" is in fact all we see, and the scene should be written as such: "Sally starts to pour the tea, but drops dead, still clutching the teapot."

- "Bob turns with a huge grin on his face." Or: "Sally's facial expression shows amusement." Can a grin, or any other facial expression, be anywhere besides on a face? Stick with "Bob turns, grinning" and "Sally looks amused."

- "Sally stands there in her pajamas." Or: "Bob stands there, confused." Where is "there"? It has to be in the location where the scene is taking place, right? Forget "there." These might seem nitpicky, but the point is that you, the writer, need to know exactly what you want to describe, and stick to it.

Keep it clear

Whatever your personal writing style is—just-the-facts or let-me-paint-you-a-picture—the action should be written in short, staccato beats with plenty of paragraph breaks. Never write your action in long, dense blocks; not only will this make your reader skip over much of what you wrote, but it will also make many people whose job it is to read scripts all day physically and emotionally very upset. Keep it simple, light, direct and to the point.

Most importantly, especially for writers who tend toward longer descriptions, don't write anything that we wouldn't see or hear if we were watching the scene. In other words, no mind-reading. For instance, if you've set up the story so that Marsha doubts that Jim is telling the truth, do not write: *Marsha doubts that Jim is telling the truth*. We don't know what Marsha is thinking unless she does or says something to reveal it. In fact, your tools as a writer are very similar to the tools an actor can use: You can only show the subtext and emotion of a scene through dialogue and the characters' expressions, gestures, actions and dialogue. If Marsha responds sarcastically to Jim, if she storms out, if she throws a television at his head—all these things will show us her emotional state.

DIALOGUE

It's not only important to write *good* dialogue, it's also important to format dialogue correctly so that it is easily located by the actors and clearly readable for everyone.

The dialogue column is indented on both sides of the page. It is basically centered, with a few tweaks. The character name is close to center (this will vary slightly in different script formatting software; Final Draft places the character name 3.5 inches from the left page margin and 7.25 inches from the right). The dialogue itself starts on the line below the character name, and is wider on the page than the character name. This column is also nearly centered (in Final Draft, 2.5 inches from the left page margin, and 5 inches from the right). Within this column, the dialogue is justified on the left margin. This means that the letters line up in a perfect vertical line, just like the left margin of a book or academic paper. The dialogue's right margin is not justified; it will be ragged. A good way to check whether you've done this right is to ask yourself whether your spoken dialogue column looks like a book (correct), or whether it looks like centered poetry verses that spread to unequal lengths on both ends (incorrect). For example:

> JIM
>
> Marsha, I'm telling you I love you! You're the only one I've ever been able to talk to. I'd die if you ever left me.
>
> MARSHA
>
> For some reason, I doubt you're telling the truth.

Dialogue begins with the name of the character who is speaking. The name is *always* capitalized. Important rule: Always call your character the same thing. If you have an actor playing a character called Ski Bunny #1, then that actor is going to scan every scene for dialogue labeled Ski Bunny #1. If the writer starts calling that character Cute Ski Bunny or Ski Bunny Girl, then the actor is going to ignore those lines because they appear to belong to a different character.

Following the character name, you'll drop down a line and begin the dialogue itself. Occasionally, you might add a *parenthetical*. The parenthetical is a direction or a bit of action that appears directly under the character name and above the dialogue. It is nearly centered (in Final Draft, 3 inches from the left page margin, 5.5 inches from the right).

Be sparing with the parentheticals because they are often used incorrectly as a way to tell us what the characters are thinking, instead of expressing those thoughts in the action or dialogue. This is an example of "mind-reading," or how a parenthetical should *not* be used:

> MAN
>
> (very happy about his promotion)
>
> I just had a really good day!

Why is this bad? As mentioned before in the action section, writers can only communicate to the audience things that can be heard or seen. Yes, the audience may see that a character is happy, but they can't know his exact state of mind or the reasons behind it. The audience never sees that parenthetical in the script, so how will they know the character is happy about his promotion? The writer has to establish that the character got a promotion and make sure that the reason for his happiness is visible or audible in the scene (e.g., he tells someone, frames his promotion letter).

Ideally, the story context and the *lines themselves* should tell us everything we need to know. Most good dialogue requires no parentheticals at all. Parentheticals can be dangerous if they become a crutch, or a way for a writer to feel like the emotion of a scene is clear when actually it isn't being communicated effectively to the audience. Only use parentheticals when it's logistically necessary for the scene. For example, if there is more than one character in the room, sometimes a parenthetical can be used for clarification, like so:

              JIM
        (to Dave)
How are you?

             DAVE
        (to Sam)
I'm fine, thanks.

             SAM
        (to Dave)
I wasn't the one asking.

             DAVE
        (to Sam)
I know, I'm not talking to him.

             SAM
        (to Jim)
Why isn't he talking to you?

             JIM
        (to Dave)
Tell Sam I'd rather not speak to him right now.

TRANSITIONS

Often overused by new screenwriters, transitions are a way to tell the director and the editor how you want the scenes to be cut together, and it's something they'd rather you didn't tell them. That said, much like parentheticals, transitions *can* be used properly.

The most used transitions are: CUT TO, DISSOLVE TO, SMASH CUT, FADE IN and FADE OUT. Here are some basic rules for using them:

- **CUT TO:** Use only when it's completely necessary and essential to your plot and story to cut from one scene to the next at that particular moment.

- **DISSOLVE TO:** Used to show the passage of time (memories or flash-forwards). Also used to create a sentimental, nostalgic or sad effect.

- **SMASH CUT:** A smash cut is an aggressive, fast cut used often to show a change in emotion, or something blowing up, or for comedic effect. It's not recommended to use this transition often, as, again, it's one of those things that will be worked out during shooting and editing.

- **FADE OUT:** The end of a script.

Now that you know the terms and how to use them, we'll do what every good screenwriting book does: we will share a sample script, in its entirety. This script was produced and can be seen online (www.leapyear.tv, Season 2, Episode 1). See the appendix for a breakdown of the sample script followed by the script itself.

Copyright

In the business of online series, creators often have to wear many different hats: producer, director, actor, cinematographer and, of course, screenwriter. There are, however, aspects of the process that aren't so much creative as necessary. Filmmaking is by nature collaborative, and a finished work can have many different authors. Because authorship comes with a specific set of rights, it is extremely important to educate yourself about the legal issues that may affect your work even before you create it.

Before we go any further, let us discuss an important point of the law: *The copyright to a work for hire always belongs to the employer, not the employee, when the work was created in the scope of his or her employment.* If you were hired to write and/or produce a web series, the copyright will always belong to whoever hired you, unless otherwise specified by a contract. For example, even though two of the authors of this book wrote the web series *Leap Year,* they do not own the copyright because they were *hired* to do the work. On the other hand, as independent creators of *Break a Leg,* they own the copyright to that series and all of its related materials.

Because the latter is by far the most common scenario for a web series, this chapter will focus on the independent creator and not the creator of a work for hire.

Please note that *none of the information here is intended as legal advice.* Its purpose is to provide a starting point for research and to gather in one place the kind of knowledge that is useful to an online content creator. Always keep in mind that you're swimming in largely uncharted waters, and there are many legal grey areas best navigated by a professional. Likewise, while the information presented in this chapter is applicable in the United States, your content will reach a global audience and you may not enjoy the same protections in other countries. (That is not to say you will have fewer protections; depending on the country, you may actually have more. The point is they could be significantly different.) Therefore, in these and any other legal matters, you should always consult a licensed attorney for advice.

WHAT IS COPYRIGHT?

Copyright gives the creators of an artistic work certain legal rights with respect to their creations. In the United States, these legal rights are regulated by the federal government (not individual states), which is granted the power in Article I, Section 8, Clause 8 of the United States Constitution: "To promote the Progress of Science and useful Arts, by securing for limited Times to Authors and Inventors the exclusive Right to their respective Writings and Discoveries." If you're a screenwriter and you've already written your script, you are enjoying the protections of copyright law right now. A work is fully protected the moment it exists somewhere outside your brain, which means it is "fixed" in a recognizable medium. No work is copyrighted *until* it is so "fixed." Note, however, that ideas and concepts (even if they are firmly on paper) cannot be copyrighted. You can't describe a character who smokes cigars and talks exclusively backward in a concise paragraph and expect to own all rights to that character.

A copyright should not be confused with a patent or a trademark. A copyright specifically protects a work of original authorship such as a play, movie, book, piece of music, etc., but it does not protect the subject matter of the work, only the work itself. For example, if some characters in your web series discuss how to create a fully functional time machine, that dialogue is covered by your copyright. However, there's no legal way to stop another web series producer from creating a show without your consent in which the characters build the time machine based on your characters' conversation.

In contrast, a patent covers the invention of a new product and gives the inventor the right "to exclude others from making, using, offering for sale, or selling the invention throughout the United States or importing the invention into the United States." If we continue with our time machine example, patenting the time machine itself would prevent others from building the device without your consent. A written work is not considered an invention and is not eligible for a patent.

Finally, a trademark refers specifically to a word, symbol or image used in commerce in order to differentiate the source of a product from others of its kind. For example, the McDonald's double arches are a trademarked logo that differentiates the burgers sold by McDonald's from the burgers sold by other fast food companies. If you create a production company to create your web series, for instance, you may want to register your logo to ensure that it is unequivocally associated with you and your products.

WHAT ARE MY RIGHTS?

The following rights are bestowed upon copyright holders:

1. *Copying:* You have the exclusive right to make copies of the work, as well as to profit from these copies. If you create a web

series and decide to sell copies on DVD out of the trunk of your car—that's your right.

2. *Distribution:* You have the exclusive right to distribute your work (yes, including all those copies you made) and profit from the distribution. For example, if you decide to sell the high-resolution version of your show on iTunes, show the low-resolution version for free on YouTube and also give away the DVDs as party favors at your wedding—that is your right.

3. *Adaptation/derivative works:* You have the right to create or license the creation of derivative works, meaning a piece that is based on preexisting work. These derivative works may then be covered by their own copyright. Let's consider the series *Break a Leg* as an example. Suppose an unsavory network executive hated the show itself but deeply loved the concept of *Swamblers,* the parody show-within-a-show that features prominently in the *Break a Leg* world. Could said executive take *Swamblers* and put it on the air without permission from the creators of *Break a Leg?* The answer, thankfully, is no. If the executive were to create *Swamblers* as a standalone series, he would be creating a derivative work, thereby violating the creators' rights.

4. *Public performance:* You have the exclusive right to control (and profit from) public performances of your work. For example, your local grocery store cannot play your web series about bananas on all of its in-store televisions without your permission even if it's not charging anyone for the viewing privilege.

The rights granted by copyright last for the duration of your lifetime plus 70 years. This means that if you are the Mark Twain of the web series world, your family can continue collecting royalties on your work long after you've been put on a raft and shot with burning arrows.

This brings us to another one of your rights as a copyright holder: the right to give away your rights. There are times when you may want to give away your exclusive rights, and you are granted this ability under the law. For instance, at the time of this book's publication, the series *Break a Leg* is licensed by Fox Italy for international distribution. What this means is that Yuri and Vlad, the creators and copyright holders of *Break a Leg,* have granted Fox the exclusive right to distribute (and profit from the distribution of) the series within a defined geographical area and for a specified period of time. Upon the completion of the time period defined in the contract, the exclusive distribution right for that region reverts back to them.

Whether and how you give away some or all your copyrights is entirely up to you. If you want to license the public performance right of your series to a living statue on Market Street in San Francisco for a span of six hours every other Tuesday, all you need is a contract specifying those terms. Whatever you do, though, be sure to understand exactly what it is you are giving away or you may end up losing more than you thought (see Paul McCartney, Michael Jackson, Beatles catalog). It is always important to consult an attorney before entering into contract agreements.

WHO OWNS THE COPYRIGHT?

In the simple case of a single creator who produced a piece of original art without any input from others, it is clear who owns the copyright to the final product. However, in the world of film, the work is usually shared among multiple creative contributors and for legal purposes is considered a "joint work," which is defined in Chapter 1 of the U.S. Copyright Code as "a work prepared by two or more authors with the intention that their contributions be merged into inseparable or independent parts of a unitary whole." In a work-for-hire scenario, only the client (the party or parties doing the hiring) owns the copyright; in a big Hollywood production this would likely be the producer. However, in the case of independent film and web video, it is just as likely that a group of like-minded artists came together to create the final product. In that case, who owns the copyright?

First, let's consider the screenplay, which is a literary work that can be copyrighted even if a motion picture is not produced. In the case of multiple authors working on one screenplay, the screenplay itself is considered a "joint work" and all authors are co-owners with an equal share in the copyright unless otherwise specified by a contract. You may want to define specific terms in case, for example, there is a lead writer who will do the bulk of the work and should have greater control over what happens to the script. If a contract is not established, all parties contributing to the work are considered co-authors with equal rights.

When an actual motion picture is created based on the script, numerous people will be involved in the production process. Each person who contributes something copyrightable to the whole is considered a co-author. For instance, a musician who created the soundtrack for your web series has contributed a work of art that has been recorded onto a recognizable medium and can be copyrighted in its own right. The musician, therefore, is considered a co-author of the motion picture. On the other hand, Uncle Joe, who had a great idea for that one character to always wear a blue hat, is not considered a co-author because ideas are not copyrightable. Similarly, the helpful intern who brought you coffee is not a copyright holder because his contribution to the process (while significant) is not copyrightable on its own.

As mentioned above, each of the joint authors has all of the same rights as any individual author no matter how large or small his or her contribution to the final product. Any of the authors, therefore, can exercise his rights to the whole work in any manner he chooses and without having to consult with the other authors. For example, if the musician who created the soundtrack to your web series is a joint author (i.e., you did not specify otherwise in a contract and she is not your employee), that musician can decide to give away the exclusive right to distribute your web series in the United States to her grandmother without consulting you or any of the other joint authors. Note, however, that profits resulting from this arrangement must be split among all of the joint authors.

As you can see, the finer points of copyright ownership can get muddled pretty quickly. Even if it is clear who the actual copyright holders are, the question of how to exercise the rights granted by the copyright can bring an otherwise congenial group of authors no small amount of grief. Because of this, it is extremely important to create a contract with the help of a licensed attorney that specifies the rights of all parties involved prior to creating the product.

PROTECTING YOUR COPYRIGHT

As discussed, copyright is automatically established when a creative work is fixed in a recognizable medium. Proving that it was fixed by you at a certain time, however, is another matter. Imagine that you've written a web series about a super-intelligent coffee cup, and you've shown the script to a friend. Your friend, having turned out to be a spy for an unscrupulous online video channel, creates a derivative show about a super-intelligent spoon that *actually uses full lines of your dialogue* (remember, ideas are not protected by copyright, only work that exists in a medium such as a script). What will you do? Will you march into your lawyer's office waving your laptop as proof? How would you establish that you were the first to create the script? You may have heard of the "poor man's copyright," the method of mailing yourself an envelope with the copyrighted contents and using the postmark as proof that you created the work at a certain date. Don't do it. This has not held up in court. There are more legitimate methods of establishing authorship and the date the work has been created.

The best method of protecting your copyright is to register your work with the U.S. Copyright Office of the Library of Congress. You will need to provide a copy of your work, fill out some forms and pay some fees, but in the end, you will have a product that is officially registered with a government body. If anybody should infringe on your copyright, you will have an easily verified source to assist you in proving your ownership. Note that you can register both screenplays and motion pictures with the copyright office; we recommend registering whichever product will be *available to the public*. For example, if you've created an independent web series, you should register it as a motion picture to include all of the involved parts (cinematography, music, dialogue, etc.). On the other hand, if you've created a pilot script to pitch to network executives, you should register the script as your "public" product.

Another slightly cheaper option is to register your script (note: script only!) with the Writer's Guild of America. This registration will establish the date of creation, but does not provide you with any further legal rights. It is important to note that although you have copyright the moment your work is created, if you should decide to pursue a court case against an infringing party, your work will need to be registered with the U.S. Copyright Office even if it has been previously registered with the WGA. The actual registration process can be quite lengthy and can significantly delay your court case, so there's an advantage to registering your work with the Copyright Office as soon as it's created. In addition, if your work has been registered with the U.S. Copyright Office prior to the date of infringement or within 90 days of the publication, you may seek attorney fees and statutory damages as part of your lawsuit against the infringing party. If you registered only with the Writer's Guild, this option is not available to you.

USING COPYRIGHTED WORKS AND COPYRIGHT INFRINGEMENT

We've already discussed the rights that are granted to copyright holders as well as the complicated dance of who owns those rights at any given time. But it's not just your own rights that you need to be concerned with. Suppose you would like to use a previously copyrighted work in your own web series. For example, many student show creators wish to use copyrighted songs in their soundtracks, or short clips from TV shows or films. What do you have to do to make sure you don't get sued for copyright infringement?

First, find the source of the work you'd like to use. This may be as easy as doing a web search and finding all the information you

need on the creator's website, or it may take a little more digging.
You will need to research the following points:

1. *Is the work intended for public use?* Some works are created specifically to be used by the general public. If that's the case, you
   will usually be able to find some kind of a license agreement on
   the creator's website that outlines the terms of use. Be sure to
   carefully follow these terms. For example, if the creator gives
   you the right to use her work on the condition that your project
   will be available free of charge to the public, be sure you are able
   and willing to adhere to that condition *forever.* While your web
   series may start out for free on YouTube, you may want to sell
   DVDs one day, which would violate the above agreement.

2. *Has copyright expired?* If a work was published before 1923,
   the copyright has expired and the work is in the public domain.
   If a work was published between 1923 and 1963, you should
   check with the U.S. Copyright Office to see if copyright has
   been properly renewed. If it hasn't, the work is in the public domain. You may use a work that's in the public domain without
   having to ask for permission from the author or his family.

3. *What are the licensing terms?* If a work is not in the public
   domain and you would still like to use it, you should determine
   what the terms are for licensing it. Even if the work is by a
   major artist, the licensing fees may not necessarily be out of
   reach. Don't be afraid to ask the artist's representative; you may
   be surprised at his willingness to negotiate an agreement that
   is acceptable to all parties involved.

If the work is not in the public domain, you generally have to
secure permission from the copyright holder to use it. There is an
exception to this, which is called "fair use." This doctrine outlines
some cases where a copyrighted work may be used in some form
without getting permission from the copyright holder. The fair use
doctrine is frequently misunderstood and misapplied, and under-
standably so; the legal language and court precedents are legion and
almost incomprehensibly intricate. There is a common (and incor-

rect) belief that students can use up to 30 seconds of any audio or video material as long as it's for a class (i.e., for educational purposes). Fair use usually covers matters such as book reviews that include direct quotes from the book, or teachers using copyrighted material to educate their students in a nonprofit institution. Fair use can also apply to both satire and parody, though courts have been more inclined to grant the protection to parodies. The key thing to know is that the burden of proving fair use rests with the person accused of infringing on the copyright. Therefore, unless you are prepared to defend your position in court, be very careful with assuming you have fair use rights.

COPYLEFT AND CREATIVE COMMONS

In recent years, an "anti-copyright" or "copyleft" movement has evolved within the open-source software community and spread to the realm of creative works. The main purpose of copyleft is to allow the free distribution of a work while ensuring that any derivative works remain in the public domain. As the GNU (an open-source project of the Free Software Foundation) website states: "Anyone who redistributes the software, with or without changes, must pass along the freedom to further copy and change it." This ethos also applies to "copyleft" protection of creative works. You can choose copyleft by using the GNU General Public License or Creative Commons' ShareAlike license.

As we have discussed, copyright has been refined by the courts to ensure that artists have full control of what happens to their creations. In contrast, the purpose of copyleft is to ensure the free exchange of ideas and to encourage collaborative creation. When you create a work under copyleft, it must be distributed without charge. Furthermore, it is expected that others will create derivative works, which can include direct contributions to the original project, use of parts of the work in other projects and creation of whole new works based on the original (e.g., sequels, prequels). These derivative works can be created, copied and distributed by other parties without the consent of the copyleft holder. The only condition to the copyleft license is that all derivative works must be freely available under the same license.

For example, if you create a copylefted web series, other creators would be able to contribute episodes to the series and to use any material from your original episodes without your consent. However, these creators cannot charge money for the performance or distribution of their derivative work, nor can they deny free access to their episodes to other creators who may in turn want to create further derivative works. (How meta!) Similarly, if you would like to contribute content to a web series created under copyleft, you may do so with the understanding that your contribution must be freely available to anyone who wishes to view and/or modify it.

Note that copyleft does not mean that you've abandoned the copyright on the content you've created. What it means is that you are using your copyright in a particular way to grant rights to others with respect to your content. Without copyright, you actually couldn't create the terms of copyleft, which is essentially a form of contract that defines how your work may be used by others.

If you are not already familiar with the Creative Commons licenses, check them out. The website clearly lays out the elements of copyright that you can choose to retain, withdraw upon certain conditions or decline altogether. It also lets you generate the exact license you want (and even gives you a graphic to use). For instance, choosing an "Attribution/Non-Commercial/Derivatives OK/Share-Alike" license means that anyone may use all or part of your work as long as they credit you for the original material, do not sell or make profit from the derivative work, and make their derivative work equally accessible to others (i.e., don't put a more restrictive license on their work than you did on yours). Creative Commons licensing has been adopted by many college and university media, cinema, music, theater, fine arts and creative writing departments as official department policy. Students are highly encouraged to learn about and use these licenses as well, even if their ultimate choice is to retain full copyrights.

Creative Commons also provides many links to sites where you can easily find CC-licensed, public domain, copyleft and other "safe" audio and video material to use in your own works. In addition, don't forget there are lots of aspiring musicians and bands out there who would love to create an original score or theme song for your show—that's a great way to support other artists while you begin your own career.

CHAPTER 9

Production

Your script is done; the structure is tight, the dialogue flows and everyone who's read it can barely contain their applause. What's next? One of the best parts of working in the online space—you can make your show for an actual audience.

There are, of course, restrictions, and by that we mean money. Budgets for web shows are increasing and likely will continue to do so. That said, very few brands, networks or producers want to invest money in an unknown commodity, and no matter how good your script is, you are for now unknown. Therefore, the first step in getting a budget is to create something without one. This is your chance to demonstrate your abilities and create a visual résumé for yourself so that potential brands and investors can see what you can do. You never know—if you put your little unfunded project online and it gets a million views, well then, that's even better.

Production isn't easy, of course, especially without a budget. This chapter provides a quick-and-dirty look at getting the job done.

PRE-PRODUCTION

Pre-production is where the work really begins. This is when you build your main team, find your crew, cast your actors and create your shooting plan. Pre-production is incredibly important to every project, so take your time and get every possible detail nailed down before you begin shooting.

The Must-Have Crew

You need a group of people who'll take on your script and do it justice in turning it into a web series. Without money, your crew, their abilities (and yours) and your chemistry with one another are essential to creating a great product.

Your first job is to find your high council, so to speak. Most writers don't know much about production, which means you have to find a team that does. Here are the bare minimum positions you will need to fill.

Producer

Typically, the producer makes everything happen. She hires the crew, oversees production and helps the writer's vision come to life. In many web shows, the writer/creator is also the producer, but it doesn't have to be that way. Know your strengths; if you're a good organizer and you understand how film works, then by all means, produce. Otherwise, find someone you can absolutely trust to do it for you. Not only does the producer need to see this project as the unique and fragile creature that it is and believe in you as a writer; she also has to be trustworthy and have a personality that melds with yours. Your producer is going to be your closest confidante, your partner in this venture, so pick one carefully. Remember, if you find a moral, dedicated and talented producer, that producer will naturally find a moral, dedicated and talented crew.

Director

The director runs the production and transforms the script into a visual, living, breathing thing. While the producer is the boss, the director leads the creative process; think of the producer as the head of the navy, and the director as the captain of the ship. You should work closely with the director in pre-production, figuring out what the feeling of each scene is, what the character motivations are, etc. Never work with a director who thinks it's best to cut the writer out of the production; that's backward thinking, and it often ends poorly. That said, don't be an overbearing writer. You've chosen this director because you believe in his vision, so let him *have* a vision and trust him to make the best final product possible.

Director of photography (DP)

An unfortunate fact about web series is that they tend to be less than impressive visually. A talented DP can change that and put your show ahead of the rest. The DP works closely with the director and often the writer to help tell the story through compelling, well-chosen and well-executed imagery. On a no-budget production, the DP will also often be the cameraperson. If you're *very* lucky, the DP will also bring his or her own camera gear.

Production manager

Your production will live or die in this person's hands. In film and TV shows, the production manager handles the budget and schedule and reports to the main bosses. In an unfunded/independent web show, the production manager does almost everything. He makes the schedule, communicates with the actors, helps find locations (and in rare instances of a tired and spaced-out director, locates his misplaced glasses, script, etc.). On a no-budget set, everyone has to wear several hats and the production manager tends to wear the most. He is also often underappreciated, and if there's a hang-up, he is first in the line of fire. So treat your production manager well, because without him, your show will soon feel like a train careening off its tracks.

Other Essential Crew

The essential crew are the folks who will carry out the mission of actually manifesting the final product. These are the absolute essential people you need to make a shoot run:

Boom operator

Would you give a camera to someone who has never filmed anything before? Probably not. And yet, the boom microphone is often given to whoever has a free hand that day. This is why most web series have terrible sound. A great boom operator can maximize the sound quality of every scene. An amazing boom operator will bring her own gear to make that sound *perfect*.

Editor

An editor is extremely important to a series because you can't have a finished episode without editing what you film. The editor cuts and arranges the raw footage into a coherent, tight, satisfying story. Think of the editor as the last person in the writing relay. There are three very important questions to ask when you're appointing an editor:

1. Do you get along with her? You and the director will work in close quarters with her throughout post-production, so make sure you click.

2. Is she good at editing? An editor can make a bad project decent, a good project great and a great project terrible, depending on skill and sensibility.

3. If you're making a comedy, is she naturally *funny*? Don't assume that every good editor is good in the same way; they all have individual senses of humor. Comedy is a game of timing, beats and moments. An editor needs to feel all of that in the very core of her being and be able to nail those moments in the editing. Choose carefully.

Production assistants

Life is just easier with production assistants. Production assistants are the people who do everything from getting coffee for the actors and crew, moving lights and helping with props to periodically being an extra in a scene. Production assistants are necessary in a bare-bones crew because at a certain point, you need extra hands. The good thing is, they're easy to find. Many of your fellow students would kill for a chance to work on a real set and gain experience, and you would kill to have them help you.

The Dream Crew

The previous two sections describe the most bare-bones team you need to make your series. In web-show production, a small team can achieve a lot with very little. The trick is to find the right people. In a team this small, all members have to pull their weight and be capable of multiple jobs. Not only that, they also have to love the project, believe in the project and have personalities that click with yours and everyone around them. Assembling the right team will be one of the hardest parts of production. But if you get a group that truly clicks, real magic can happen.

That said, there are important jobs that if you *can* find good people to do them will not only make your life a thousand times easier, but will also increase the quality of the production as a whole.

Sound editor

You can have a great boom operator, but you're still going to need a sound editor in post-production to get the sound as perfect as it can be. In many indie productions the editor also does all the sound work. Sometimes this is adequate, but often the editor won't have the right gear or knowledge to optimize the sound you've recorded or to re-create sound that was recorded poorly, perhaps inaudibly. If you find a sound editor willing to work with you for cheap or free, scoop her up before she has a chance to change her mind; she will be an absolute godsend.

Assistant director (AD)

The assistant director acts as a go-between for the director and the rest of the team. He also makes sure that the set is running efficiently, that no one is slacking and that people are hustling to get work done. It's a hard job that requires an intimate awareness of every aspect of the production and the composure and organizational skills to make sure everything is running smoothly (with help from the production manager). In many ways, the AD is the bad guy on set, the one who tells people to stop having so much fun and get back to work. It's not a pleasant job, but it's a necessary one, and a good AD can speed up production immensely.

Gaffer

A gaffer is responsible for the execution of the DP's lighting setup. In some cases, the gaffer actually helps design the lighting as well. On a lot of no-budget productions, the DP is also the gaffer, camera-person and grip. However, the fewer jobs the DP has, the better she can focus on her own work. A good gaffer can make the set run significantly faster *and* make the footage look much more professional.

Key grip

The key grip is the head of the grip department and often operates camera gear such as cranes, dollies and so on. The grips will also sometimes help the gaffer set up the lights. On many sets, this job will be done by whoever is free at the moment. But if you can get yourself a grip team, you'll find life is not only easier, it's also *safer.*

Grip

These are the key grips' lackeys, and the more of them you have, the faster your production moves.

Camera operator

This person relieves the DP of having to concentrate on camerawork, enabling him to make sure the overall picture turns out gorgeous. Having a few camera operators can be really helpful and conducive to a better end product.

Assistant camera (AC) operator

This person builds the camera in the beginning of the day, takes it down at the end of the day, and is also the focus-puller (the person who makes sure the image remains in focus). Can the camera operators do these jobs themselves? Mostly, aside from some of the focus-pulling. Does it make their lives a million times easier to have an AC on hand? Yes, yes, a thousand times, yes.

Hair/make-up artist

It might seem vain, unnecessary and in most cases definitely expensive, but the prettier your actors, the better the footage. Keep in mind, your actors are the ones being stared at and scrutinized by the viewers; the least you can do is make sure they look their best. It can make a striking difference in the overall look of the footage when a hair/make-up artist does up your talent, and it's one of those touches that gives your series that professional polish.

Wardrobe

Much like make-up and hair, wardrobe is often overlooked but incredibly important. Many low-budget producers just tell their actors to grab something from their closet. Sometimes this works fine, depending on the actors' fashion sense and the contents of their closet, but ordinary clothes look really *ordinary* on screen. Even if your script calls for grungy clothing, the costume needs to be assembled with some skill and an eye for detail; remember, clothes make the man, even if that man happens to be a bum. A costumer's job is to get your actors to look like the *characters* they're playing, not like themselves in their regular attire. Wardrobe also needs to be designed with the entire cast in mind, as well as the look and style of the overall production, rather than one character at a time. Lack of attention to wardrobe will make your production look cheap (which it might be, but you don't have to let it show).

Script supervisor

The script supervisor's main job is to make sure what you're shooting can actually be cut together in editing. He makes sure scenes are being shot at the right time of day, the right lines are being spoken and the actors' movements are consistent in each take. In particular, he makes the *editor's* life a thousand times easier and often acts as the director's and DP's right-hand man.

There are many more jobs on a production than we've listed here, of course. Most film crews are gigantic beasts, with every position having its own union and every person filling a specific and specialized job. An indie crew is often much smaller. It's a trade-off, though; the indie filmmaker will always have a tougher time creating a series with high production values. On the other hand, they're far more capable of shooting guerilla-style and getting shots and locations that a bigger production would have to pay thousands of dollars to get.

The Cast

Good actors can make bad footage look good and average writing sound brilliant. The same can be said in reverse: Bad actors can kill the best production values and annihilate a genius script. Be patient in choosing your talent, be critical, know what you want and don't settle for anything less.

Finding actors

Generally, the casting director's job is to find you your dream cast, but alas, you probably won't be able to afford one. The job then falls to you, your producer, your director and your production manager.

There are many ways to find actors. Post ads on Craigslist and local acting-job listing sites. Visit your local theaters, colleges and universities and ask if you can post listings on their boards (if you don't ask first, they might get taken down). If you need child actors, approach school principals (not teachers), who can in turn talk to parents.

Keep in mind that your friends might be very nice and probably fun to work with, but they aren't necessarily good actors. Many web-show creators rely on their buddies to act in their series, which might work out fine if it suits your content. But by the time you've gone through the real work of pre-production, you'll find that you've raised the bar and are more concerned with the overall quality of your show. Casting inexperienced actors or non-actors can tank a show, even if everything else is top-notch. Audition *everyone*—friends included—and be honest with yourself and them. You're going to spend hours and hours working on this project; don't sell it short because you want to have fun with your friends.

If you can't pay the actors, find other ways to entice them to audition; for instance, the chance to work with a DP with a nice reel or on a project with a terrific script will go a long way toward getting more experienced actors to work with you.

Auditioning

Auditions are not only a chance for you to check out actors; it's also a chance for them to audition you. They will be gauging your level of professionalism (and whether it's worth committing to your project, especially if they are working for free). Don't hold auditions in your living room. Find a clean, private, appropriately furnished location that says you and your team are taking this project seriously. This will also motivate the actors to put *their* best foot forward in terms of their performance and their personal interaction with you.

You're trying out to be these actors' creative guide and "boss," and they are deciding whether they'd like to work with you or not. They are checking out your communication style, basic know-how, congeniality, sense of humor, sense of purpose, etc. The more communicative, open and professional you are in the audition, the better chance a higher caliber actor will want to join your team.

Keep in mind that auditions are incredibly tough for many actors. Even for experienced performers, trying out can be a nerve-wracking process, so treat them well. Be kind, understanding and courteous. Give them some direction to start with and be open to seeing what happens; they might actually give you new ideas and reveal things you didn't fully know about your characters, story and more.

Pay

You're probably not going to be able to pay your actors with actual money, so the standard is to offer them meals, copy and credit. This means that you will feed them at every shoot, give them a copy of the series when it's done and put their names in the credits. It's the very least you can offer, and the very least most actors will work for.

Equipment

Chances are you're starting with very little equipment, if anything at all. Luckily, technology has made filmmaking a whole lot easier in recent years with the invention of the DSLR camera. Many current filmmakers use the Canon DSLRs, which look like regular digital cameras but have fantastic video modes that will give your footage a real professional quality. One of the most affordable is the Canon EOS Rebel T2i, which provides great video quality for an incredibly low price (under $800). Lenses can be expensive, but if there's one thing to throw money at, it's your camera gear.

Everything else you can probably get by begging and borrowing. Sometimes, the crew will have their own gear. You might want to invest a bit of your own money in equipment you can own and use for years. The best two things to own are a camera and a good boom microphone. Lights are crucial but expensive; you can cheat and get clamp lamps and china balls, which are good for soft lighting. While not ideal, these will provide the minimal amount of light needed for a professional-looking scene.

All in all, while equipment is definitely getting cheaper, it's still quite hard to obtain amazing production values without spending any money. So keep your equipment restrictions in mind when you write; make it seem like you *chose* to shoot with lower quality gear to make the world feel a specific way.

Planning the Shoot

When you have no money and a small crew, it's important to know exactly what you're shooting and how you'll shoot it before you get to the set. That way you can foresee potential problems and figure out solutions for them before they derail shooting.

Here are several basic elements to put together before you start production:

Shot list

Your director and DP will create the shot list, which breaks down every scene into the separate shots needed to put it together in editing. This isn't necessarily something you'll participate in, but depending on your control-freak rating, you might choose to sit in on these meetings.

Storyboards

You've probably seen professional storyboards in which an artist draws out every frame of the film in consultation with the DP and the director. Your team might work on something similar to accompany the shot list. Storyboards are a great way to visualize the script before spending time and money shooting it, so we highly recommend that you put one together.

Several programs are available to help you storyboard, all of which are expensive. FrameForge's Previz Studio (starting price around $400) lets you create full 3D versions of your locations and characters, and move them around at will. This software is incredibly useful. StoryBoard Quick (priced around $250) is a bit cheaper and easy to use. But again, you're spending money that could be used for craft services, a new boom mic, or any number of essential on-set necessities. So what's your best option as an independent filmmaker? A well-sharpened pencil and a nice, firm piece of paper. You don't need to draw to make a good storyboard; stick figures and circle-men make splendid avatars for your actors, and as long as it's clear to you and your DP what you're trying to convey, then you're in business.

Locations

Many web series creators don't put much stock in locations, which is unfortunate, because locations are one of those little details that can make an amateur production look professional. Locations can be easy to come by (though in L.A., where everyone is making a film, you might be expected to pay for permission). Ask a hundred stores, bars and friends until someone agrees to let you film for free or cheap. Offer to put the business and/or business-owners' names in the credits, offer hugs, offer food—offer whatever you have, because if there's one thing that really makes a series look *good,* it's the right locations. If your series doesn't specify seedy or downscale environments, try to aim for high-end locations. For instance, don't just place your characters in a bar or a gym or an office; go for *nice* ones. Consider the location's colors, textures, lighting. It will add *a lot* of polish to your visuals.

Shooting schedule

Once you have your shot list done, your storyboards drawn and all of your locations chosen, it's time to make a schedule. This is where a good production manager will make your life infinitely easier. Be realistic about what you can shoot in a day and how many locations you can cover. It's generally realistic to expect to shoot five pages in a day, but you might manage a lot more than that. While a 10-hour day is standard (but hard) and a 12-hour day is not uncommon (but even harder), you may be dealing with actors who have other commitments, such as classes to attend or jobs to go to. If you're pushing your unpaid cast and crew too hard, you will soon lose them to exhaustion or desertion. The other problem with doing too much in one day is that the scenes start suffering. If the director, DP and actors aren't getting the time they need to perfect every moment, it'll show in the final product.

Not working for a brand or a network gives you one major advantage—no time limits on shooting (unless you are working on a project for a class)—so use that. Take your time, make sure every scene shines, and it'll pay off in the end.

Props

You most likely will not have a prop master, so have your production manager make the list of props you need for every scene and start assembling them with everyone in the crew and cast. Apply the same philosophy to your props as you do to your locations: Go for high-end when you can. Real is better than fake; new is better than used; repaired and repainted is better than shabby. Like good locations, good props will lend polish to the overall look of the show. Many college and university theater departments have prop rooms; thrift stores are also a great place to find cheap props and costumes.

When pre-production is complete, you should be able to look over all of your plans and have a solid idea of what you're shooting, when you're shooting it, how you're going to shoot it and with whom. Suspending production to solve problems that could have been prevented in pre-production is a huge drag (and puts you in danger of losing a disappointed, frustrated or just plain busy cast and crew) so take your time and *don't start until you're absolutely ready.*

PRODUCTION

The best part of a production is, well, the production! This is where you get to see your words finally come to life. Take a moment to look around on your first day—all these people have come together because they believe in *your* project. Be grateful, be happy, be determined and be stubborn, because the next several weeks are going to be a mixture of sheer joy and pure hell.

The following are some ideas to keep in mind during production; hopefully, this foreknowledge will help you maintain your (and your team's) sanity.

Everything Will Go Wrong—And That's Okay

Well, not always—but often and in very surprising ways. People will get sick, locations will explode, props will be lost and cameras will break. Be comforted in knowing that this happens to everyone; from the smallest of film sets to the biggest productions in Hollywood, there's something about film shoots that makes them a target for medium- to high-level disasters. In Tim Burton's *Charlie and the Chocolate Factory,* a $540,000 lens fell into a vat of chocolate, destroying it completely and temporarily halting production. This happens, so learn to love all of it.

Don't Panic

This is not only good to know during production, but a great thing to practice in life, too. Given the dictum "everything that can go wrong *will* go wrong," the real question is, how do you handle it?

Many filmmakers panic, throw tantrums and break down, which helps nobody. From the beginning, you and your main crew should agree on one thing: If something goes wrong, the first response from *all* of you should be, "How do we fix this?" Remember, everyone involved in your project is spending valuable time and energy working on it. When things go wrong, they look to you and your main team for guidance—so guide. Trust that there is a solution to everything. And believe in miracles; every so often, the solution turns out better than the original concept.

Be a Team

It's something we all learned in elementary school, but it still applies to filmmaking: Be a team. You're all trying to accomplish the same thing, so work together, compromise, talk, be honest and, perhaps most importantly, leave your egos at the door. Leadership is important, and things fall apart fast when no one is willing or able to make executive decisions. But when possible, don't pull rank on your people.

Be Good

There are countless production horror stories about sets riddled with difficult or negative personalities, particularly on the main team. This makes sense, because the main team is in a position of power, and everyone feels lousy working under a bad boss. You're not paying anyone, so make your set not only efficient but *fun*. Make the relationships familial; care about your crew and actors; treat everyone equally and well. Be *good* and maintain that kind of behavior the rest of your working life. So many people in this business have been traumatized by the many terrible personalities in it that they will naturally gravitate to the honest and the good. Be that person and you've already got a leg up.

Feed Everyone

If there's one place where you have to spend money, it's craft services, which is a fancy way of saying *food*. It's your duty to feed your actors and crew, and it's the very least you can do for them when they're spending hours working for you. Even though it's cheap and convenient, try to stay away from greasy, sugary, stomach-churning foods. Get healthy food for your people; it shows that you respect and value them and that you want them to have a good experience working with you. It also helps keep bodies and brains working properly (the last thing you need is a cast and crew sugar-crashing after lunch). So stick to healthy, energy-rich deliciousness—it'll pay off on those long, exhausting days and nights of shooting.

Have Fun

Not only do you get to play pretend, you also get to see your art produced in front of your eyes, so enjoy every crazy, unpredictable, highly stressful moment of it.

No class can truly prepare you for your first shoot, so stay alert and learn from every success and every failure. As you transition from shooting to post-production, talk to your cast and crew and ask yourselves: What could we have done better? What did we do right? How do we make the next production even smoother and more successful?

Once you've got that settled, take a deep breath, pat yourself on the back and dive headfirst into the last part of making your series . . . post-production.

POST-PRODUCTION (EDITING)

When most everyone else has gone home, the editor's job begins. As a writer, you might not have much of a hand in the editing process, because this is usually left to the editor, the director and sometimes the producer. However, sitting in on the editing sessions might teach you more about writing than all the books and classes you've read and taken.

Editing will give you a whole new perspective on what you did right and what you did wrong as a writer. You know that scene you swore was perfect? Well, seeing it in post-production may make you realize it's far too long and clunky. How about that scene that you kind of hated because it never quite landed? Well, it may suddenly end up being perfect, hilarious and everyone's favorite moment. Editing lets you see your scripts in a much different way. You'll see where your dialogue sounds too wordy, you'll see where your structure falters and you'll see which jokes work on screen and which fall flat.

So shadow your editor, watch her work, listen to her complain, ask questions, show interest and learn. It's not a glamorous job, but in many cases, the editor can tell your own story better than you.

For those of you interested in editing, several programs are available. The three most commonly used are Apple's Final Cut Pro, Adobe Premiere and Avid. For the past several years, Final Cut has been a standard for independent filmmakers. However, many professional editors believe that Apple's latest edition, called Final Cut Pro X, has simplified the program so much, that it is now less suitable for prosumers. The decline of Final Cut has led to the rise of Adobe Premiere, a good alternative for the indie filmmaker. That said, the industry standard has been and continues to be Avid. Avid is more expensive and a bit less user-friendly, but if you're considering a career in editing, Avid should be your program of choice.

As with most art, you have to *do* production to *learn* production. You can take film classes, read books and listen to people who've done it their entire lives, but you really won't get the full learning experience until you've actually shot something. You've got to bleed and sweat for your work, and then you can look back and realize how little you knew before you started.

As a writer, when you get to see an entire group of people come together and put weeks of their time into bringing your words to life, it is a unique and amazing experience. It'll be everything: terrifying, exhilarating, validating, nerve-wracking and one of the most exciting things you've ever done. When it's all clicking, when everyone is working and enjoying themselves, when production is moving along like magic—very few things can compare to it.

10

Reaching and Engaging Your Audience

You've created your masterpiece. You've written, rewritten and rewritten the script; you've found actors who'll work for free; you've begged for, and borrowed (and hopefully didn't steal any) equipment; you've filmed this thing, cut it together and put it up for distribution all over the Internet. You sit back satisfied and wait for the views to roll in. What's this? Five views on YouTube in the last week? Grandma must have finally sent out that forward!

There is a lot of content on the Internet. It is not enough to add to the pile and hope for greatness. Jaded viewers click on a link, watch 30 seconds and go on to the next video of a puppy gently licking a baby. What will truly differentiate your show from everything else is creating a thriving, consistent brand and a dedicated community that flourishes around your unique work of art. This chapter discusses the process of building your show brand, creating a community around it and ways to keep the community thriving.

CREATING AN ONLINE HOME

Your video could appear in many places on the Internet. Video sharing websites, dedicated websites, embedded links on social networking websites, e-mail, blogs and news stories are just a few of the options. In the case of serialized content in particular, it is important to give your show a place where viewers can congregate to view new episodes, discuss plotlines and stay in touch with the creators. This section will discuss a range of places to host your content and compare the tools they offer to grow your community.

Video Sharing Websites

The first and obvious choice for a place to put your show is a video sharing site. Most of the major sites will let you create a page dedicated to your content and allow for some customization of colors, graphics, etc. Putting your video on one of these sites is quick, easy and doesn't require an investment in hosting and professional web design.

Most sites have useful tools to help you see how your videos are doing. These might include view counters, lists of sites that link to your content and statistical information such as the average amount of time viewers spent watching each video. Social networking tools are common as well. Features such as subscription capability, friend lists, comment sections and some form of messaging can be found on most video sharing platforms. Finally, many of the sites now have ad revenue sharing programs. This means that as your videos grow in popularity, you could potentially make money from the ads shown on the site.

A few examples of video sharing sites are YouTube, blip.tv, Vimeo, Miro and Veoh. There are many others and they are quite different in terms of the type of community they attract, editorial rules and types of videos available. Some, like YouTube, are intended for a mass audience with videos of many different types and genres with very loose editorial control of content (most of the focus is on removing obscene or copyrighted material). Other sites are more specialized; for instance, SchoolTube caters to K–12 students and is heavily moderated to ensure the content is appropriate for children.

Terms of Service

Look carefully at the various sites and read their Terms of Service (TOS) agreements in order to determine whether your video is a good fit for what the site offers and the kind of community it attracts. Let's look at the Terms of Service for SchoolTube as an example. In it, we see the following:

> You acknowledge and agree that SchoolTube may terminate and/or suspend your access to any portion of the SchoolTube Service should you fail to comply with the Terms and Conditions or any other guidelines and rules published by SchoolTube. . . . Please be aware that the majority of the content found on or through SchoolTube is for general audiences, and content should meet local community standards, but may not fit yours. Content is uploaded by Teacher moderators that follow local community standards, and STN code of ethics and standards for K–12 video broadcast.

This TOS tells you that access may be terminated if you don't follow the guidelines. It also gives a general idea of what the guidelines are. The videos should follow the SchoolTube Network (STN) code of ethics and standards for K–12 video broadcast, but the content may vary somewhat depending on community standards. Don't assume that just because you've heard a certain word or phrase on TV that you can or should use it in your work.

You acknowledge and agree that SchoolTube relies on its teacher moderators, who are not employees of SchoolTube, to screen or review published content on the site to determine whether it contains false or defamatory material, or material that is offensive, indecent, objectionable, or that contains errors or omissions. This section lets the reader know that the site is moderated and it's entirely up to the moderators to determine if content is "offensive." Also, you can't sue SchoolTube if your content gets deleted because these moderators are not its employees. Finally, the following section goes into more detail on the definition of *offensive:*

> You agree that you will not use SchoolTube services to . . . upload, post, email, otherwise transmit, or post links to any Content that is unlawful, harmful, threatening, abusive, harassing, tortuous, defamatory, vulgar, obscene, pornographic, libelous, invasive of privacy or publicity rights, hateful, or racially, sexually, ethnically or otherwise objectionable.

This definition is very broad and may, for example, include any shows that use profanity (i.e., *vulgar, obscene*). In fact, the last phrase *otherwise objectionable* leaves the power to determine what *objectionable* means in the hands of the moderator. If a moderator finds your main character's blue hair objectionable, for example, the terms of service give the moderator the legal right to remove your content.

This, of course, is an extreme case. This site is meant for students and teachers to share videos, and as a consequence it has to limit the content to what's appropriate for a K–12 audience. The main point is that reading the terms of service is a great way to make sure you're posting your videos to a site that's right for your series.

Dedicated Websites

A dedicated website gives you ultimate control over your content. You are the administrator and you make the rules; it's your own editorial policy; you have total control over the amount of advertising shown; and there's no forced "standard" look to your pages. In addition, a skilled web designer can add unique community features to your site that aren't available elsewhere and that can help differentiate your product from others. For instance, should you want to create a multiplayer online game set in the world of your show, your only constraint would be your budget.

Most hosting providers offer visitor statistics similar to what you might get from the video sites, but with even more detail. For in-

Co-authors Yuri and Vlad on finding the wrong audience

Early in its life *Break a Leg* won a contest and became a weeklong featured show on Metacafe, a popular video sharing site. Sounds great, right? What we didn't anticipate was that this was not the type of video that Metacafe visitors expected. *Break a Leg* was a scripted, full-length sitcom with seven-minute episodes. Most of the content on Metacafe, on the other hand, featured kittens stuck in things, babies falling over and people getting severely hurt in hilarious ways—mostly unscripted home videos under 90 seconds. Needless to say, *Break a Leg* did not get a lot of positive reviews.

On the other hand, when we joined Blip.tv—a site specifically designed for serialized, scripted content—the response was much better. The site's community expects to view longer, scripted shows, and as a result, *Break a Leg* was well received by the viewers and frequently featured by the editors. The lesson we learned was that it is extremely important to explore the site you will be using to host your show before you spend your time building a community there.

stance, in most cases you should have access to full logs showing what visitors did on your site and which country they came from. This type of information can be extremely valuable in determining which portions of your site are particularly interesting to people (and which are less popular) and even help determine the direction of your show. For example, if your site is regularly visited by users from Italy, you might want to add an Italian character or even translate a whole episode into Italian for your loyal fans.

The biggest disadvantage of hosting your show exclusively on a dedicated website is the fact that you are solely responsible for building the show's community. Without the built-in community of a video sharing or social networking website, it becomes difficult—though by no means impossible—for anyone to find your content (more on self-promotion later). In addition, a dedicated website involves expenses such as hosting, domain registration and web design fees.

Social Networking Sites

Unlike the video sites, the primary focus of social networking sites is to facilitate social connections, and this means that there are good tools for fan interaction. Some of these sites even have video hosting capabilities, although these are usually not as advanced as the tools available on sites dedicated exclusively to video.

Research what's available before picking one or more social networking websites as homes for your show. Some well-known sites are Facebook and Google+, both of which have the necessary tools for video hosting and community building and are extremely popular worldwide. However, although these are the more popular sites, they may not necessarily be the best choices for your particular show if the show is aimed at a niche audience.

In addition to the more general audience social networking sites like those above, there are many highly specialized sites. Depending on your show's style and themes, these sites could be an even better place to build a community. For example, VampireFreaks is a social networking site for members of the goth subculture. This site allows for the creation of community web pages (lovingly referred to as "cults") dedicated to particular projects. If your show appeals to goths, a site like VampireFreaks would be a top choice to host your community page for the reason that everyone on the site is a member of your target audience.

Finally, not all social networking sites are well suited for video distribution and community building. Some sites focus only on individual pages, others focus on particular art forms (e.g., photos) and don't allow videos and still others have strict rules defining acceptable content. Always check what the particular site's policies are before creating your community, or you may end up with a deleted page and lost content.

Choosing the Site

As you can see, each place to host the community for your project comes with its own set of advantages and disadvantages. It is likely that your approach will change with time; the key is to choose the combination of community and video hosting services that is right for your project at each stage in its growth.

Of course, with so many different options available to host your show, the temptation is to choose "all of the above." That's not a bad approach, provided you have the resources to maintain it. As the show's audience grows, the demands of maintaining a community get bigger and bigger, leaving the overworked and underpaid creator with even less time to devote to working on the show. For this reason, a better approach becomes something like "a combination of some of the above, changing over time."

Making choices

Break a Leg's initial community home was MySpace, which did not have video hosting capability at the time. As an alternative, YouTube was used to host the videos with links to the videos then posted on MySpace. The MySpace community eventually grew to several thousand fans, so the blogging and messaging tools available on the site became important for keeping in touch with the fans.

As time passed, *Break a Leg* was featured on YouTube, which, depending on several factors (for instance, having the word *sex* in your episode title), can give you hundreds of thousands of views over the course of one day. YouTube subscriber numbers grew very quickly and we suddenly had our hands full responding to comments using both platforms. We tried to combine the two communities into one, but our pleas on YouTube to "come talk to us on MySpace!" did not yield the results we hoped for.

One reason for this reluctance was that in order to be fully involved in the community the viewer had to have a MySpace account. Many YouTube viewers did not want to bother signing up just to communicate with the creators. Another reason was that the feature set of MySpace was limiting. The available tools let us talk to our fans, but the fans' ability to talk among themselves was very minimal. As a result, if a few days passed without a new blog post, there really wasn't much of a reason for anyone to come to the *Break a Leg* page.

As this was happening, we began exploring other ways of promoting our show and had syndicated *Break a Leg* to several other places, including blip.tv, iTunes and Veoh (more on syndication later). We tried to maintain a presence on these websites as well, but the reality was that we just didn't have enough time to keep up with all of the different threads of conversation happening across all of these platforms.

CREATING A BRAND

*T*he purpose of a brand is to differentiate your product from others of its kind. With millions of faceless videos on the Internet, what gives your show the unique identity that makes people want to watch it?

A well-defined brand has many components, most of which are best left to a marketing textbook. The bottom line is this: Create a brand that reflects what your show is, and the right people will watch it. Create a confusing, inconsistent brand, and enjoy low views and lots of hate mail from people who thought your show about sex-starved vampires was supposed to be a charming romantic comedy.

As a writer/creator, your main goal should be to create a place for fans to visit that reflects the world created in your script. The feel of your show should be evident in the milliseconds a viewer's eye needs to take in the page upon which the show resides, whether this is the show's website, YouTube page, Facebook page, etc. This immediate evaluation is a coping mechanism that the Internet user develops as a response to information overload.

One good example of a web show brand is *The Guild,* a comedy about online gamers that is one of the most successful shows ever on the Internet. Visitors immediately know both of these things when they visit *The Guild*'s web page (www.watchtheguild.com). The show is described as "A web series about a group of online gamers: Over 65 million served!" The viewer perceives the identity of the show—it's very popular and it's pretty geeky.

Cartoon characters in medieval war gear are the dominant image on the site. They're in the About section, they're on the site's merchandise and they are part of the show's opening sequence. Pictures of the real actors can be found as well, but they are not as prominent on the site. Even the About section is dominated by cartoon representations of the characters.

This choice of cartoon vs. real images is an important design choice for the brand. *The Guild*'s comedy is based on the characters' fantasy world clashing with their real life. Scenes set in the gaming world are animated, establishing it as a fantasy in the context of the show, and the art design itself—similar to a children's book—screams comedy. In addition, the cartoon characters look like the human actors, creating the link between the fantasy character and the human being controlling it. The exploration of this link is a key theme in the show.

Consider what would happen if the cartoon images were replaced with images of real medieval warriors or even the actors in costume. In the first case, the feel would be entirely different, suggesting a serious fantasy epic along the lines of *Lord of the Rings*. In the second case, the images would imply a kind of dress-up play, whereas what the show wants to convey is that this world can be its own separate reality for serious gamers.

Another example is a show called *The Burg* (www.theburg.tv/). One of the first web shows, it helped to define the genre and prove that online video can be used for storytelling and not just as a kitten showcase. *The Burg*'s website also features a prominent tagline: "Who says gentrification isn't funny?" Through this simple question we start to understand what the show is about. Add the spray-painted brick wall background and we've learned something about the show in seconds: It's a comedy about gentrification.

An interesting top-level menu item on the site is "Bands." Given that such a prominent portion of the site is devoted to the show's music, we can anticipate that music plays a large role in the show. Quickly looking at images of the bands featured in this section, we understand a component of the show's identity is hipster culture. Just as the creators use music to establish the show's atmosphere in each episode, so did the website designers use the images of indie rock bands to define the brand.

Break a Leg Branding

We took a similarly deliberate approach to branding the *Break a Leg* site (www.breakaleg.tv/). The show is about a Hollywood TV writer, and this "writerness" is a major theme on the site. The background wallpaper consists of script pages (if you look closely enough, you will find the actual text from the script of *Groommates, Break a Leg*'s fictional show-within-a-show), "the sitcom" in the logo rests on a highlighter yellow background and the announcement of a season finale in progress is paper-clipped.

The creators of the shows described above try to establish a unique identity for each of their projects using visual cues of images, words and colors. These visual cues are designed to reflect the concepts of each show, quickly inform viewers of what they're about to see, and create a "face" for the show—a set of visual elements that establish the show's identity in the repeat viewers' minds. This identity is what's known as a "brand," and it is what serves to differentiate your show from other content on the Internet. Even if you don't have your own dedicated site, most video hosts let you design the aesthetic interface for your channel, page, etc., which is a large part of branding.

GROWING YOUR AUDIENCE

Say you have chosen a home for your show and it has nice colors and graphics. You even have an episode posted. An episode that is going to be seen by . . . whom? As with any endeavor, starting from scratch is daunting. Your only audience members in the beginning are the friends and family of the production team. This is a great place to start, because one of the first steps is to create the initial impression that someone is watching the show. Make sure they know about and are visiting your site and your show. After all, if you click on a YouTube video and it has only three views, how seriously do you take it? This raises the crucial question of how to get the word out about your show.

Social Network Expansion

As was mentioned earlier, a huge advantage of social networking sites is their arsenal of community tools. We know that social networks connect you to your friends, but more importantly they connect you to your friends' friends—people who don't know you and who are therefore much more likely to actually watch your show objectively and keep watching it because they enjoy it and not just because they feel a sense of obligation.

The great thing about social networks is that content can spread very quickly. A site like Facebook lets people easily share links to videos and when a video goes viral the result can be thousands or millions of views and subscribers. However, the site's popularity and the amount of content floating around can also work against you. Unless your show has extremely broad appeal, a lot of people won't even bother watching, much less pass it on to others in their network.

There are ways to get around this. As in the earlier VampireFreaks example, joining a social networking site with a narrow focus can help the show spread much more effectively. If even a small percentage of members pass the show on, they're passing it on to a group of people who are members of your target audience by virtue of belonging to this type of site. This means that even one re-post from a friend can result in many other re-posts down the line.

On the other hand, in your network of 200 on Facebook the few goths who catch your link in their ever-shifting news feeds may or may not watch it. If they do and they like it and re-post it, the link will once again get lost in their much larger general social network, effectively fizzling out pretty quickly.

Another approach is to add an individual touch. Depending on the social network you're using, you have access to many people who aren't too far removed from you and whom you could potentially contact individually. Perhaps your show is about knitting and your friend Bob's Aunt Betsy lists knitting as her sole interest on Facebook. She may not be your friend yet, but you'd likely be able to add her with a message telling her about your great new show. But please note: While it is valid to contact Aunt Betsy directly to let her know about a show that might catch her interest, sending a mass email to all of Bob's friends is not; that is called spamming and will earn you a mailbox full of hate.

Contacting people directly is, of course, much more time-consuming than the "post it and hope it spreads" approach, but could potentially yield much better results. You're getting to know people on a personal level and this kind of interaction makes a potential viewer much more inclined to give your show a chance. Also, as people start to re-post the show within their own social networks and the snowball starts to roll, the time spent contacting strangers decreases significantly. It's that initial push that takes a lot of effort.

Syndication

Syndication is essentially a way of distributing your video to many different video sharing sites by uploading it to a single site that distributes to the others for you. This may seem magical, which, of course, it is.

Video syndication sites each have their own model of doing business. Examples of companies that provide syndication services include TubeMogul.com, blip.tv and heyspread.com. Some of these services are free and some charge based on complex calculations; as with all online services, read the user agreement carefully. Another important thing to keep in mind is that these sites don't all syndicate to the same places, so it's up to you to make sure that the sites you want your video to appear on are supported. As with social networking and video sharing sites, the best way to find the right syndication service for your project is by a thorough Google search.

The main thing to know is that syndication can give your show exposure in many different markets. A popular syndication service might upload your video to YouTube, where, yes, the whole world could potentially see it, but it might also upload it to a site that's well-loved by Indonesians. This would give you exposure to a narrow market that you normally wouldn't have reached yourself. Most of the syndication services will also give you the option to choose the sites your video will appear on, so you can skip the ones you know are not appropriate for your type of content. These services will also usually provide analytics across all of the platforms you distribute to, giving you the big picture of where and how much your videos are being viewed.

One disadvantage of syndication services is that it becomes extremely time-consuming to keep up with the social activity across all of the different platforms. Since the goal is to build a community for your web series, you certainly lose potential viewers who may like the show but, not seeing any other activity around it, move on to something else. This can be somewhat remedied by referring to your community home page within the video description fields on the site, as well as inside the videos themselves (in the show's intro sequence, for example). Visiting the community home is still an extra step for viewers to take, but if they really enjoy the content, they'll be willing to take it.

Getting Featured

The holy grail for any web video creator is getting featured. This means that the social networking or video sharing site you've put your show on has decided that your video is an example of the ultimate in videos. This kind of glamour can be dangerously heady stuff. More importantly, getting featured can result in hundreds of thousands— even millions—of views for the featured video and, with some luck, new fans and community members.

Please notice the words *can result* in the above sentence, as opposed to *will definitely result*. First, many factors are involved. What time of day was the video featured? On which site? Is it a category feature or a front-page feature? Weekday or weekend? What's the video's title? The latter is actually an important consideration. An intriguing title can mean a huge difference in the number of views. For instance, the three most viewed *Break a Leg* episodes were called "High Treason," "Sex Ed" and "Sex and Violence." Note the popularity of the word *sex* (though, interestingly enough, the top-viewed video was "High Treason"). Second, you have to brace yourself to take the good with the bad. With mass exposure will come the inevitable critics and "haters." You need to develop a thick skin.

All these concerns aside, getting your show featured is great publicity. The question is, how does this happen? On most sites, the editors search for new content themselves, often noticing videos that have been getting a lot of attention. As with social networking, though, a little personal contact can go a long way. Try contacting the site's editors; ask them what it would take to get your show a featured spot or offer to volunteer in the site's community.

Even if nothing concrete comes out of it, the editors will be aware of your existence, which greatly increases your chances of being noticed for a feature spot. The important thing when making these contacts is to show that you are an involved member of the community interested in more opportunities, not just a stranger demanding a favor.

Conferences, Lectures and Community Events

The world of scripted Internet content is surprisingly small, and a great way to get more exposure to diverse audiences is to meet other content creators in person. Although, as a writer, you might prefer to communicate on the page rather than by talking face-to-face, the reality is that networking is almost mandatory if one is to succeed.

There are several big web videoconferences now and more are likely to appear in the future. The Digital Hollywood conference, held in several cities around the country, is an excellent example, as are NewTeeVee, held annually in San Francisco, and the DIY Media Festival in Los Angeles. Other events include the Streamy Awards, a web video awards show; parties thrown by technology companies involved in web video (e.g., YouTube, blip.tv); and lectures and appearances by well-known content creators, whether held at your local college or video store, or huge events such as Comic-Con and FantasyCon.

What can these types of contacts yield? Let's say you meet a creator who has a successful show about zombies while you're still working on your knitting masterpiece. How about a crossover episode? Zombies crash a meeting of the knitting club and mayhem ensues. Viewers of both shows get exposure to a new series and some may stick around and keep watching. Or another example, you wander around the convention hall and suddenly see the name tag "Bob Jones, YouTube." You walk over, introduce yourself and have an actual conversation with an editor from YouTube. This face-to-face contact is much more effective than email, because these people get thousands of messages a day.

As you attend more of these events, you will begin to see the same faces. People will know you as that guy or girl who's working on the surprisingly clever knitting show that recently took a turn for the undead. You'll recognize the other people there and begin to build relationships. These relationships in turn will yield more opportunities and exposure. It's a relatively small community, and people generally want to see each other succeed.

MAINTAINING YOUR COMMUNITY

What makes your show a destination on the Internet? The first and obvious answer is your show. Unless you're prepared to release daily episodes, however, chances are that you'll need more to keep people coming back and staying immersed in your show's world.

Consider a TV example. A few years ago, a writers' strike stopped production on most serialized shows for several months. This was followed by the usual summer TV hiatus. Upon the return of scripted television, viewer numbers were down considerably. The problem is that as people get taken out of their viewing routine, they're no longer immersed in the show's world, no longer waiting to see what happens next. When the show comes back, the motivation to keep watching isn't urgent and the show loses some of its audience.

The advantage of being on the Internet is that other types of content can keep the viewers engaged in the show's world. If your show has a thriving community, keeping this community active becomes extremely important in order to maintain an audience for your series.

Extra Video Content

For the independent creator, many factors affect the production of a series. Actors have other commitments, locations are suddenly only available at odd hours or not available at all, borrowed equipment is needed elsewhere, etc. As a result, running a full-scale production of the show's main episodes is not always feasible. During such lean times, smaller, easy-to-shoot content can be a great way to keep the viewers engaged in the show's reality, maintain the show's community between episodes, add an extra dimension to your show's world and even create hype for future content.

Minisodes

Minisodes are shorter, simpler episodes of your show. If a regular episode of the show usually has a main plot along with one or two subplots, a minisode would likely focus on one primary plot. In addition, minisodes are usually standalones, meaning there are stories set outside or in addition to the show's main plot and character arcs. The minisode shouldn't change the characters significantly or affect the development of the show's main timeline. Instead, the goal should be to provide some new insights into the show's world or characters that add to the feeling of immersion for the dedicated fan. The idea is that if a viewer only wants to follow the main arc, she won't be confused if she missed what happened in these extra episodes.

"David's Bad Day"

A *Break a Leg* minisode called "David's Bad Day" (https://vimeo. com/48816708) takes place the week before the events shown in the show's pilot. The basic plot is that a despondent, jobless David finds out that his girlfriend has been cheating on him. When things can't seem to get any worse, David gets a phone call that leads to his moving to Hollywood.

This episode is completely standalone—you can watch every *Break a Leg* episode and never need to know how David got to Hollywood. For dedicated fans, however, this episode revealed some extra information about David's character. It also gave them something to watch while we took time off the web series thrill ride to work real jobs and have occasional conversations with our families.

An important consideration for us when writing these minisodes has been to keep them within as few locations as possible and to only use readily available actors for the shoots. The goal is to maintain your community in the absence of the "main" show through minimal production time spent on the extra content. For example, "David's Bad Day" takes place in two easily accessible locations—a local café and a relative's office. There are only two characters, one of whom is Yuri, the minisode's writer. This minisode was written, shot and edited in the span of two days.

Conversations

These are exactly what they sound like: single-scene videos set in the world of your show, which have an arc that is resolved in the span of a conversation between two characters. They can be an alternative to the more demanding needs of shooting a minisode. A good practice is to keep the setting in one location and aim for roughly TV scene length, meaning two to three pages long. The goal is to give some extra insight into the show's characters in a format that lends itself to quick production. For instance, in the span of time between *Break a Leg* seasons, a new conversation was uploaded roughly every week. See the example "jen-avenge" at https://vimeo.com/47461364.

Keep in mind that conversations may not work well for every type of show. This format was particularly suited to *Break a Leg,* for example, because it was a talky comedy. A funny scene with fast dialogue is something *Break a Leg* fans were interested in seeing; the lack of plot or story movement was not a huge problem. On the other hand, a conversation set in the world of an action show may not be as appealing given the prevalence of pacing and plot. It would likely also not be as easy to shoot.

Other In-World Clips and Shorts

These are usually short scenes that help expose some aspect of the show's world to your audience. This could be a news report about a major event that influences the show's reality, an advertisement for a character's business or a music video from your main character's favorite band. Unlike the other types of minisodes, these usually don't have any real story or character arcs. The main point of these types of clips is to add depth to your characters' world.

Staying In Touch with Your Audience

An important way to maintain the show's community is to interact with fans. Creators who put in the effort to interact with the audience will find that the show's fan base is much more inclined to stay involved if they see that the people who make the show are present as well. Furthermore, your words are another form of content and therefore another reason for the audience to come back to your site and to stay connected to the show's world regardless of the availability of new videos. There are many useful tools for staying involved with your audience.

Blogs

Regular blogging on your show's website is a great way to keep your community informed of the latest developments as well as to provide some insight into the show's inner workings.

Writers can discuss the direction of the show, editors can talk about the technical aspects of the production and actors can post acting tips or even blog in character. Blogs can help you create yet another dimension for the world of your show and is content that can be generated by any member of your team.

Message boards

Dedicated message boards can be a huge boost for a show's community. Audience members can discuss aspects of the show with each other or just talk about the weather. This kind of interaction is crucial to maintaining an active community. The connections that your audience members make with each other around your show are yet another reason for them to come back and keep watching.

It is good practice for the creators to stay active on the message boards as well, not just to keep in touch with your audience but also to allow the audience to participate in the show's direction. For example, the writer might create a thread with a question: "Bob is in love with Jennifer. As we all know, Jennifer is married. Should she leave her husband for Bob?" You may or may not use any of the resulting suggestions, but you will definitely stimulate discussion. This gives your audience a sort of "co-creator" connection to your show, and yet another reason to come back.

Comment sections

These days comment sections are a standard feature of blogs, video sharing sites, social networking sites, etc. This means that wherever your show appears, you can chime in on the discussion that happens around it. Of course, at some point, it gets overwhelming to keep up with all of the sites where your show can be viewed. If your show is syndicated, chances are you won't see all of the comments your show generates unless you spend significantly more time reading comments than actually working on your show. This aside, it is good practice to occasionally find some of these sites via a general search engine and contribute to the discussion. You never know what may come from this type of interaction.

This chapter gives you a glimpse into the new media world that your show will live in. Unlike traditional television, your content will not appear before a voiceless audience provided by unknown cogs in the big studio machine. As a writer for one or more web series, your role will likely include PR, marketing, web design, tech support and a million other jobs that don't necessarily have anything to do with writing. This sort of workload can be overwhelming, but it can also be extremely rewarding. You get to decide where your show lives; appeal to the kind of people who want to watch it; and ultimately become a member of a community dedicated to the world you conceived, created and produced. This freedom to produce and distribute as you see fit is what makes the online world an appealing choice for content creators.

IN CLOSING . . .

In the end, you can read this book a hundred times (go ahead, we dare you), but the fact is, to truly learn your art, you must do it. There is no better school than your own set, no better book than practice and no better teacher than experience. We've hopefully given you the tools to begin your, dare we say, adventure—but it's up to you to take these tools and make something great.

As we said before, everything may go wrong. Money will run out, locations will be lost and your kind-of-real prop sword will inevitably get stabbed into your actor's leg. Learn from it. Embrace it. Some people spend their lives working in an office all day—you'll be making movies. Aside from being a rock star, is there anything better?

So, go forth and create. Tell stories, make worlds, create, create, create and, above all else, enjoy the hell out of it.

Appendix

LEAP YEAR, Episode 1, Season 2

On the following pages you will find a copy of the actual script, reproduced page for page. The notes below describe the script's various sections and their purposes. You may want to read through this breakdown before reading the script, or you may want to flip back and forth as you go. (The page numbers referred to below are those in the upper right of the boxed pages.)

BREAKDOWN

A good first episode of any series (and of any season within that series) has two structural jobs: the first is to create a good, strong first episode. The second is to set up the action for the rest of the season and to ask the *season's* central question. This is why a first episode is often the hardest to write.

PP. 1–2, COLD OPEN

On the web, getting your audience's attention in the first couple of minutes is key. We wanted to start the second season in a way that would get the attention of not only the people who watched season one, but also new viewers. Having Eliza Dushku in the first shot didn't hurt either.

Aside from grabbing attention, the cold open of a first episode is like the opening of a movie—it should be indicative of the rest of the story. Introducing June Pepper at the very top did just that—not only is she the villain in the first episode, she's the villain for most of the season.

PP. 3–11, ACT I

▪ The first scene in Act I almost immediately accomplishes the job of a first act—we meet our characters, and we're introduced to the central question for the episode: Will Jack save the day?

▪ The flashback scene in Jack's house has two major purposes—the first is to catch up new viewers with what happened last season. The second is to show that Jack is going to be the CEO of C3D. This plot point not only helps up the stakes of Jack's disappearance before the interview, but also sets up Jack's entire season arc.

▪ The end of Act I should raise the stakes, turn the action in a different direction and remind us of the episode's central question. Jack handcuffed to June's couch does just that: he seems completely unable to get to the interview (stakes raised), now the others have to figure out what they'll do without Jack (direction changed), and we're still wondering: Will Jack get to the interview and save the day (question asked)?

PP. 12–18, ACT II

▪ Act II is the journey part of the script, where characters are further developed as they try to solve the main conflict. The first scene, between Jack and Aaron, sets up their relationship and shows us Aaron's very real fears of both moving to San Francisco and Jack leading the company.

▪ Still cuffed, Jack's unfortunate situation punctuates Aaron's worries and keeps raising the stakes.

▪ As the gang arrives at What's Trending, they're coaching Aaron on what to say. The Act II turning point often comes in two beats, the problem (Jack still cuffed), and the apparent last ditch effort. Aaron seems a poor replacement for Jack—which is why, near the end of the scene, a very unprepared, still-cuffed Jack shows up to "save the day." It seems like the central question is answered—but saving the day is more than just showing up. Jack is sorely unprepared—so the stakes are still high that he doesn't mess it all up.

PP. 19–25, ACT III

- Act III starts us into the climax, and the clicking red heels bring us back to the very beginning—who is June? Was her handcuffing Jack really a result of fooling around? Or is there more? Aside from Jack being unprepared, we re-introduce the original element—an enemy for C3D.

- Jack shows off his charm and gives us a reason to be on his side, even though his actions are going to cost the company dearly.

- We know something bad is going to happen, and the shady guy in his shady car continues to build the action.

- Jack continues to charm Shira Lazar and sets up the real meat of the climax...

- The fact that thugs destroy the office answers our central question: Will Jack save the day? Apparently not. But it gets worse.

- Jack's tryst with June not only gets the C3D office destroyed, it also means he didn't get to look at the notes Olivia wrote up for him. As mentioned previously, Episode 1 must also ask the central question for the entire season—in Leap Year's case, the question is: Will the C3D team pull off their launch successfully? And it's asked right here, in the climax.

- The prototypes are stolen, and now that we know the central question, the stakes have gotten very high.

- Jack tells Shira that the launch is in "3 months" instead of the 9 months that Bryn and the rest of the team actually need. No prototypes and a crazy deadline make things almost hopeless—and, hopefully, even more gripping.

DENOUEMENT

The denouement in this episode is a bit unusual. Whereas a regular denouement is the resolution, in Leap Year it's a flashback to the moment where Jack finally convinces Aaron to trust him, and come to San Francisco to work on starting C3D. After all that happened in the episode, it's an ironic foreshadowing that helps underline the drama of the last 18 minutes.

<u>LEAP YEAR</u>

"A Train Wreck"

Season 2
Episode 1

by

Vlad and Yuri
Baranovsky

Happy Little Guillotine Films

COLD OPEN

1   INT. SAN FRANCISCO - BAR - NIGHT   1

A SWANKY bar. A PRETTY GIRL laughs at something a MAN says to
her -- they lean casually against the BAR WALL, behind them,
text hangs on the wall.

TEXT: PRESENT.

JACK SATHER leans against the bar, FINISHED DRINK still in
hand, trying to focus desperately on several pieces of paper
in front of him.

A VERY GIRLY DRINK slides across the bar. Several people look
surprised as it slides past them. Jack grabs it at the last
second.

Jack slowly picks up the glass as a woman -- JUNE PEPPER --
leans on the other side of him.

                    JUNE
          Nice catch.

                    JACK
          Your throw?

                    JUNE
          My throw.

                    JACK
          Nice throw.

                    JUNE
          Nice...
               (looks him up and down)
          ...face.

She stretches out her hand.

                    JUNE (CONT'D)
          June.

                    JACK
          Jack.

They shake hands.

                    JUNE
          So, what's a girl like you doing in
          a place like this?

LEAP YEAR, S2, EP. 1 "A TRAIN WRECK"   2.

>   JACK
> Being emasculated, apparently.

>   JUNE
> Well, you can't blame me, can you?
> You come into a bar dressed like
> that, you're practically begging to
> be hit on.

>   JACK
> I'm studying --

>   JUNE
> For your psychology finals? Yeah.
> How about this, Mr. Jack. How about
> you and I get into your car -- I'm
> assuming you have a car?

>   JACK
> I have a... big car...

>   JUNE
> Great. How about you and I get into
> your "big" car, go to my place, and
> enjoy the night in a way that very
> few people really let themselves
> enjoy a night. And then, in the
> morning, when I kick you out -- and
> Jack, I *will* kick you out -- you
> can go to a coffee shop or a
> basement or wherever it is you do
> the thing that you do, and, while
> doodling almost creepily detailed
> doodles of our doodly wedding, you
> can go ahead and study your little
> heart out... how about that?

Jack looks at her for a long moment, slowly takes a sip of
his very pink drink.

>   JACK
> June, I know it's early, but... I
> think I'm falling very deeply in
> love with you.

He pulls his keys out, smiles and...

ROLL INTRO.

                        <u>END OF COLD OPEN</u>

LEAP YEAR, S2, EP. 1 "A TRAIN WRECK"   3.

ACT I

2   INT. OUTSIDE OF C3D OFFICE - HALLWAY- DAY   2

AARON MORRISON walks swiftly down the street, phone in hand.
In his other hand, he holds A CONTAINER with TWO COFFEES.

> AARON
> (into phone)
> What do you mean he's not in? It's
> one thirty in the -- I'm almost
> here. In San Francisco -- what do
> you mean where? I'm almost at the
> office. Has no one called him? I
> said *has no one called him?*

Aaron gets to the front doors of the C3D OFFICE. He pushes it
open and walks inside.

3   INT. C3D OFFICE - LOBBY - DAY   3

Aaron walks up to their FEMALE SECRETARY -- SARAH, 28 -- and
puts his phone down for a moment.

> AARON
> Hey, Sarah, has Jack been --

> SARAH
> No, everyone's asked already.

> AARON
> Yeah. Sorry.
> (into the phone)
> Weren't you *with* him last night?

OLIVIA walks in.

> OLIVIA
> Who, Jack?

> AARON
> Yeah.

> OLIVIA
> I had dinner with him.

> AARON
> I thought *Bryn* --

LEAP YEAR, S2, EP. 1 "A TRAIN WRECK"   4.

                         OLIVIA
               I had dinner with him, I gave him
               the bullet points, we talked about
               diets, everything was great.

She walks by Aaron and he follows her deeper into the office.

4   INT. C3D OFFICE - HALLWAY - DAY   4

Olivia walks swiftly, Aaron trails.

                         AARON
               And?

                         OLIVIA
               And we agreed that having a cheat
               day seems pointless -- on Saturday
               I had a four cake lunch, let me
               repeat that, a *four cake lunch* --

                         AARON
               I was still on Jack.

                         OLIVIA
               Oh, I have no idea where he is.

                         AARON
                    (into the phone)
               Olivia has no idea where he is but
               she had a lot of cake. You texted
               him?

5   INT. C3D OFFICE - MAIN ROOM - DAY   5

Aaron and Olivia walk by BRYN, who works busily on a bunch of
computer parts. She's also on the phone.

                         BRYN
                    (into the phone)
               Yes, I've tried every type of human
               contact with the man and it's like
               trying to get the Pope on the --

They stop in front of her.

                         BRYN (CONT'D)
               Phone. The pope on the phone.

She hangs up.

                         AARON
               Hi, Bryn.

LEAP YEAR, S2, EP. 1 "A TRAIN WRECK"   5.

He gives her one of the coffees.

>   BRYN
>   Hi, Aaron.
>   (to Olivia)
>   Did you bring cake?

>   OLIVIA
>   This was on Saturday. I can't have
>   cake any other day.

>   BRYN
>   But Saturday is Cake Day?

>   OLIVIA
>   It's a thing.

>   BRYN
>   *Every* Saturday?

>   OLIVIA
>   It's starting to feel like that.

Derek walks in.

>   DEREK
>   I've looked in all of his favorite
>   sleeping places and I can't find
>   him.

>   OLIVIA
>   This isn't great for us. What's
>   Trending is in a few hours.

>   DEREK
>   What's Trending?

>   OLIVIA
>   That's right.

>   DEREK
>   No, I'm asking you.

>   OLIVIA
>   Yeah, I'm *answering you*.

>   AARON
>   Okay, Abbot and Costello -- it's an
>   online talk show.

>   BRYN
>   A huge online talk show.

                              AARON
                    If you ever read your email, Derek,
                    you'd know Jack was supposed to be
                    announcing the date for our product
                    launch on What's Trending today.
                    But no Jack could mean no interview
                    and...
                         (beat)
                    I knew this would happen.

                              OLIVIA
                    What?

                              AARON
                    This. This was exactly my problem
                    with coming here.

                                                        CUT TO:

6   INT. JACK'S HOUSE – NIGHT – FLASHBACK   6

Olivia, Bryn, Jack, Derek and Aaron all sit around a table.
Jack is standing in front of a whiteboard that's covered in a
SHEET.

CHYRON: NEW YORK, FOUR MONTHS EARLIER.

                              JACK
                    Just hear me out.

                              DEREK
                    I'm in, regardless.

Behind them, the BEDROOM DOOR OPENS, and a GIRL in a MEN'S
SHIRT walks sleepily out of it, and into the KITCHEN. No one
notices except Jack.

                              AARON
                    You're in because you want to run
                    away from the girl suing you for
                    religious discrimination.

                              DEREK
                    Maybe. Or maybe I *believe* in us.

Aaron glances at him.

                              DEREK (CONT'D)
                    Okay, more the lawsuit thing.

LEAP YEAR, S2, EP. 1 "A TRAIN WRECK"   7.

                    JACK
          If we say yes, we have half a
          million dollars to work on a
          revolutionary product --

                    OLIVIA
          Yeah, with *Andy Corvell* as our main
          shareholder. You remember him? The
          guy who *fired* us to teach his other
          employees lessons on business.

                    DEREK
          Not to mention his little spy,
          Bryn.

                    BRYN
          I said I was sorry. Unlike you, who
          stole my *server* --

                    OLIVIA
          Yeah. We obviously have a strong
          foundation here.

                    JACK
          Regardless of the issues, we're
          friends and we're good at our jobs.
          You guys wanted to run a successful
          business? You wanted to be
          entrepreneurs? You wanted to be
          your own bosses?

He removes the sheet off the whiteboard. It reads:

COO: OLIVIA

CFO: AARON

CTO: BRYN

CRO: DEREK

                    JACK (CONT'D)
          You got it. We've got have half a
          million dollars and we've got a
          gadget that will make *holograms* a
          regular part of people's lives. Is
          this something anyone in their
          right mind would say no to?

                    AARON
          And you remember the small fact
          that we'd have to relocate to San
          Francisco?

>   JACK
> No winter, the heart of the tech
> industry and we're in California.
> Sounds terrible.

>   AARON
> I have a family.

>   DEREK
> Yeah, because that excuse isn't
> getting old.

Aaron glances at him and then back to Jack.

>   AARON
> What about the CEO?

>   JACK
> What about him?

>   AARON
> He's missing on your board. And
> coincidentally, so is *your* name.

>   JACK
> Right.

>   AARON
> Right. So, that's a pretty
> important job, right? It's the face
> of this entire thing. Whoever does
> it would have a huge amount of
> responsibility.

>   JACK
> Yeah. So...

He flips the board, on the back it reads:

CEO: JACK.

Before any of them can talk, the GIRL walks back into the
room.

>   GIRL
> I can't find my pants.

They all look at her.

>   GIRL (CONT'D)
> I had this vague memory of them
> being in the oven.
>   (beat)
> But then they weren't.
>   (MORE)

LEAP YEAR, S2, EP. 1 "A TRAIN WRECK"   9.

                              GIRL (CONT'D)
                    (beat)
               My bra was in the microwave though.
                    (beat)
               Were we cooking my clothes?

They all slowly look back at Jack. Jack smiles sheepishly
and...

7   INT. JUNE'S APARTMENT - LIVING ROOM - DAY   7

Jack startles awake. Around him are what seems like dozens of
empty BOTTLES and GLASSES of various ALCOHOLS.

Jack is in his boxers. He goes to pull his arm down and
realizes that he is HANDCUFFED to the couch arm on which he's
laying.

He struggles with it for a second, then lays his head back
down.

He lays for a moment and lets his eyes wander around the
room. It's a nice place. Jack's PANTS hang on a LAMP.

Jack's eye catches a clock.

CHYRON: PRESENT, 1:43 PM

                              JACK
               Oh, god.

He slides up and tries to look for his clothes -- they are
nowhere to be found, and he can't exactly go anywhere.

                              JACK (CONT'D)
               Hello?

Nothing.

                              JACK (CONT'D)
               April? May? Septem-- that can't be
               it.
                    (beat, thinks about it)
               June! I seem to have misplaced both
               my clothes and the key to the --

June walks into the room, dressed and ready to leave.

                              JUNE
               Someone is loud in the mid-
               afternoon.

>   JACK
> Someone needs to leave your house
> and go to a pretty important thing.

>   JUNE
> And I would love to help that
> someone, but I've got my own *thing*
> to go to and there's a small chance
> you swallowed the key.

>   JACK
> Why?

>   JUNE
> I don't remember. Things got weird?

>   JACK
> Okay.

>   JUNE
> Okay. I'll be back later. Don't go
> anywhere. I've always wanted to say
> that to a tied up guy.

>   JACK
> June, this is intriguing, it is,
> but I really need to go.

She turns around.

>   JUNE
> I bet.
>   (beat)
> "Jack." Where do I know you from?

>   JACK
> I used to be a child actor.

>   JUNE
> You're in the tech industry. I just
> saw your picture in Mashable.
>   (beat)
> *Oh!* The thing. C3D. *Right.*
> Holograms. Magic. *Jack Sather.*
> You're the CEO.

>   JACK
> Weren't you supposed to kick me
> out?

>   JUNE
> I was, but you're just so damn cute
> I kinda want to keep you.

LEAP YEAR, S2, EP. 1 "A TRAIN WRECK"   11.

                    JACK
          June.

                    JUNE
          I know. You want to go. But you
          know what they say, you take a
          man's freedom, and he stays, you
          give a man freedom and he...
               (beat)
          I was hoping I'd find the joke by
          the end of that sentence.
               (shrugs)
          Okay, bye.

                    JACK
          Wait!

She looks back.

                    JACK (CONT'D)
          We had sex, right?

She smiles, shrugs, and walks out.

                    JACK (CONT'D)
          Well... damn.

                    <u>END OF ACT I</u>

LEAP YEAR, S2, EP. 1 "A TRAIN WRECK"   12.

<u>ACT II</u>

8   <u>INT. BAR (NY) – NIGHT – FLASHBACK</u>   8

Jack and Aaron sit in a bar, drinking together.

CHYRON: NEW YORK CITY, SIX MONTHS AGO.

> JACK
> I don't think they'll do it if
> you're not in.

> AARON
> That's flattering. I'm still not
> in, though.

> JACK
> You're the neurotic moral center of
> the group. We need you.

> AARON
> If you think this date is going to
> end with my pants in your oven,
> you're wrong.

> JACK
> I got you a present.

> AARON
> What?

> JACK
> I got you a going away present.

> AARON
> Okay. Except I'm not going away.

Jack puts a large box on the counter. Aaron stares at him.

> JACK
> Just open it.

Aaron sighs and unwraps it. Slowly, a large golden castle
with a whiskey bottle inside of it is seen.

> JACK (CONT'D)
> It's a whiskey castle music box!

> AARON
> A whiskey castle --

Jack pulls the whiskey bottle from the center out. Music
plays.

LEAP YEAR, S2, EP. 1 "A TRAIN WRECK"   13.

                    JACK
          Music box! It plays -- Catskills
          Jamboree! No, I don't know what
          song that is --

                    AARON
          I'm not going to San Francisco and
          I'm not keeping your whiskey
          castle --

                    JACK
          Music box!

                    AARON
          Okay.

                    JACK
          Aaron, what are you worried about?

                    AARON
          Raising a son while starting a
          company. Moving away from my city.
          Lisa not wanting to --

                    JACK
          Lisa will go. If you ask her,
          she'll go. Lisa is the coolest
          thing about you.

Aaron drinks quietly for a moment.

                    AARON
          Okay. You know what I'm worried
          about? I'm worried that we take
          this huge risk, put everything
          we've got on the line, and the
          person that's supposed to lead us
          fails and everything goes to hell.
               (beat, looks at Jack)
          I'm worried about *you*, Jack.

9   INT. JUNE'S APARTMENT LIVING ROOM - EVENING   9

Jack tugs hard on the couch arm. He's drenched in sweat --
he's been at this for a long time.

His PHONE rings again.

                    JACK
          I KNOW. I *KNOW*. I HEARD YOU THE
          LAST SIX HUNDRED TIMES.

He kicks the arm on every word:

LEAP YEAR, S2, EP. 1 "A TRAIN WRECK"   14.

                         JACK (CONT'D)
          The. Thing. Is. I. Think. I. Slept.
          With. A. Sociopath!

He gives up, exhausted.

                         JACK (CONT'D)
          Aaron is going to be so mad at me.

10   INT. WHAT'S TRENDING STUDIO - LOBBY - EVENING   10

Aaron, Bryn, Derek and Olivia walk into the What's Trending
Studio -- it's big, impressive and has a lot of people
milling around.

CHYRON: PRESENT, 4:56 PM.

                         AARON
          I'm still not sure what I'm saying
          here.

                         DEREK
          I could do it.

                         OLIVIA
          You're fine, Aaron. Talk about the
          product, talk about what it does --

                         BRYN
          No one has done this before. Hit
          that.

                         OLIVIA
          Yeah, I'd throw revolutionary
          around as much as you can.

                         DEREK
          Or, again, I could just do it.

                         BRYN
          Aaron, one thing -- we're doing the
          launch in nine months.

                         AARON
          Nine months, got it.

                         DEREK
          Or just ignore everything I'm
          saying.

                         BRYN
               (to Derek)
          Done.
                         (MORE)

LEAP YEAR, S2, EP. 1 "A TRAIN WRECK"   15.

                          BRYN (CONT'D)
                     (to Aaron)
                That's important. If you get
                nothing else right, this is the
                thing you need to say -- *the
                official launch event is in 9
                months.*

                          AARON
                Okay.

                          BRYN
                Nine months.

                          AARON
                Wait, how many months?

                          BRYN
                Okay, good.
                     (beat)
                You know what, I'm going to go
                ahead and write it on your hand.

She pulls out a pen.

SHIRA LAZAR walks over to the group. She's pretty, fast-
talking and busy.

                          SHIRA
                You the C3D brigade?

                          OLIVIA
                Hi, yeah.

                          SHIRA
                Great. We're all really excited
                about it. I'm Shira by the way --

                          BRYN
                We know who you --

Shira jumps back, having not seen Bryn.

                          SHIRA
                Jesus Christ. I thought you were
                his shadow.

                          OLIVIA
                Yeah, Bryn is neck deep in laundry
                day. We're all really happy to be
                here, Shira. Your show is great.

LEAP YEAR, S2, EP. 1 "A TRAIN WRECK"   16.

                         SHIRA
              Thanks.
                   (to Aaron)
              You're Jack?

                         AARON
              I'm Aaron, I'm the CFO, Jack is --

The doors BURST open and Jack flies in. He's mildly
discombobulated but -- he's still Jack.

                         JACK
              Hey, kids, where's --

                         BRYN
              Finally.

                         JACK
                   (leaps back from Bryn)
              God! You've gotta pick brighter
              places to stand.
                   (sees Shira)
              Shira Lazar.

                         SHIRA
              You're Jack.

                         JACK
              You know when I heard I was doing
              What's Trending I thought, well,
              you know, the same thing everyone
              thinks when they hear "*web show*" I
              thought -- *gross*. But you've got a
              thing here, Lazar, you guys are
              doing something great.

                         SHIRA
              That's a terrible compliment.

                         JACK
              I also like your --

                         SHIRA
              I'm dating someone.

                         JACK
              -- ability to interview. Hm?

                         SHIRA
              We're going on in five, Mr. Sather,
              try not to be *too* charming.

LEAP YEAR, S2, EP. 1 "A TRAIN WRECK"   17.

                         JACK
          I can't promise something crazy
          like that, but I also can't promise
          to care that you have a boyfriend.

                         SHIRA
               Okay.

She walks away.

                         AARON
          Where the hell have you been?

                         JACK
          Well, it started with me working on
          all the bullet points you guys
          wanted me to memorize.

                         DEREK
               Where did it end?

Jack holds up his hand -- he's still handcuffed to a large
piece of wood.

                         AARON
               Jesus Christ.

                         JACK
          Yeah. And then I had to take a cab
          because --
               (to Bryn)
          Can you pick the lock on this?

                         BRYN
          I'm not *actually* Lisbeth Salander.

                         JACK
               Okay. Well, wish me luck!

He heads toward the studio.

                         OLIVIA
               Jack! You know what you're saying?

Jack whirls around and spreads his arms -- he has CLIPPED his
undershirt together with BINDER CLIPS.

                         JACK
               I always know what I'm saying!

He walks off. After a moment:

LEAP YEAR, S2, EP. 1 "A TRAIN WRECK"   18.

                    AARON
          I'm worried something horrible is
          about to happen.

                    END OF ACT II

LEAP YEAR, S2, EP. 1 "A TRAIN WRECK"   19.

ACT III

11   INT. SAN FRANCISCO - STREET - NIGHT   11

MUSIC PLAYS.

HEELS click against the ground. They belong to a pair of RED HIGH-HEELED shoes.

Click, click, click, they walk with purpose.

A woman in a warm winter sweater -- hood up -- plays with a yellow envelope as she walks.

Click, click, click.

> SHIRA (V.O.)
> Tell me about C3D.

12   INT. WHAT'S TRENDING STUDIO - SET - NIGHT   12

Jack talks to Shira.

> JACK
> It's Skype with holograms. You can see your parents, your long-distance lover, your kid in Afghanistan -- you can see them like they're right in front of you.

> SHIRA
> And it actually -- I'm sorry, are you handcuffed to a piece of wood?

Jack looks at his hand.

> JACK
> It appears that I am.

> SHIRA
> Care to explain?

> JACK
> Well, it's a short explanation. I lost the key.

> SHIRA
> You lost the key to...

> JACK
> To the cuffs. I lost the key.

He shrugs, she laughs.

13   EXT. SAN FRANCISCO - STREET - NIGHT   13

The WOMAN stops next to a BLACK CAR. The window opens. A MAN -
- a LARGE MAN -- sits in the driver's seat.

The Woman tosses the envelope to him.

                    WOMAN
          Tonight. Everything you need is in
          there.

                    MAN
          Got it.

He starts the car and she walks off.

                    SHIRA (V.O.)
          You've been getting some press.

14   INT. WHAT'S TRENDING STUDIO - SET - NIGHT   14

                    SHIRA
          People are definitely interested.

                    JACK
          Of course they are, C3D is the
          future of communication.

15   INT. WHAT'S TRENDING STUDIO - BEHIND THE CAMERA - NIGHT   15

Olivia, Aaron and Bryn stand behind the camera, watching.

                    OLIVIA
          He's good at talking, I'll give him
          that.

                    AARON
          Yeah.

16   INT. WHAT'S TRENDING STUDIO - SET - NIGHT   16

                    SHIRA
                    (laughs)
          Are you worried at all about coming
          off a little... sure of yourself?

LEAP YEAR, S2, EP. 1 "A TRAIN WRECK"   21.

                         JACK
              I left my girlfriend and a cushy
              job in New York City to move to San
              Francisco and spend all of my money
              on C3D. I'd be in trouble if I
              wasn't sure of myself.

                         SHIRA
              So you don't see any problems on
              the horizon?

Jack laughs.

                         JACK
              None we can't fix.

17   <u>EXT. C3D OFFICE - NIGHT</u>   17

THREE MEN - dressed all in black with SKI MASKS ON -- walk
into the C3D office.

They look around for a moment, and one holds up the bat,
walks over and SMASHES the VASE off the receptionist table.

The other two take note, and raise their own bats.

                         SHIRA (V.O.)
              Fair enough. So, when will we get
              to see C3D in action?

18   <u>INT. WHAT'S TRENDING STUDIO - SET - NIGHT</u>   18

Jack looks at her for a moment.

                         JACK
              What's that?

                         SHIRA
              When is the official launch for the
              product?

Jack looks at her for a moment and, playing it cool, glances
off camera...

19   <u>INT. WHAT'S TRENDING STUDIO - BEHIND THE CAMERA - NIGHT</u>   19

                         BRYN
              Oh, god. He has no idea.

Bryn, Aaron, and Olivia gesture -- each trying to say "9."
Aaron realizes it's on his hand and he holds it up.

20   INT. C3D OFFICE - NIGHT   20

We see two hands grab TWO C3D PROTOTYPES and throw them in a
sack.

21   INT. WHAT'S TRENDING STUDIO - SET - NIGHT   21

Jack looks at Shira.

                    SHIRA
              You okay, Jack?

                    JACK
              You've got great eyes.

                    SHIRA
              The launch party?

                    JACK
              And mind you, I don't love
              complimenting a woman on her eyes --
              it's cliche and, well, too...
              loving. I'm not ready for *loving*.
              Well, let me rephrase that --

22   INT. WHAT'S TRENDING STUDIO - BEHIND THE CAMERA - NIGHT   22

Aaron watches on in horror.

                    AARON
              This is a train wreck.

23   INT. WHAT'S TRENDING STUDIO - SET - NIGHT   23

                    SHIRA
              Jack, when is the launch party?

                    JACK
                 (beat)
              Three months.

24   INT. WHAT'S TRENDING STUDIO BEHIND THE CAMERA - NIGHT   24

Bryn, Aaron, Derek and Olivia look horrified.

                    BRYN
              Oh, god, no.

LEAP YEAR, S2, EP. 1 "A TRAIN WRECK"   23.

25   INT. C3D OFFICE - MAIN ROOM - NIGHT   25

One man FLIPS one of the tables.

A bat SMASHES a laptop.

A third man opens the doors to the SERVER ROOM. He whistles,
they all turn around and slowly walk toward it.

26   INT. WHAT'S TRENDING STUDIO - SET - NIGHT   26

                         SHIRA
              Really? Three months? That seems a
              little... ambitious.

                         JACK
              It is ambitious. The whole damn
              project is ambitious, but it'll be
              done in three months. And we're
              going to have the biggest and best
              launch party that this town has
              ever seen. Because we're New
              Yorkers, Shira Lazar, and if
              there's one thing we know how to
              do, it's throw a party.

                         SHIRA
              In three months.

Jack smiles.

                         JACK
              In three months.

27   INT. C3D OFFICE - MAIN ROOM - NIGHT   27

The four men exit out -- leaving a complete disaster behind
them.

28   INT. WHAT'S TRENDING STUDIO - BEHIND THE CAMERA - NIGHT   28

                         BRYN
              That's it. We're done. We're
              completely and totally done.

29   INT. NEW YORK - BAR - NIGHT - FLASHBACK   29

On the BAR, TEXT READS: NEW YORK, SIX MONTHS AGO.

Jack and Aaron sit in the same place, drinking.

> JACK
> You don't have to worry about me.

> AARON
> No? You sure? Because I'm pretty
> sure you're getting ready to drink
> an entire castle full of whiskey.

> JACK
> No. My whole career has been
> building to this. I can do this,
> Aaron. I won't fail you guys.
> (beat)
> Plus, I think you're already in.

> AARON
> Yeah? How do you figure?

> JACK
> Because it's midnight and you have
> a wife and a kid at home. Only
> reason you'd still be out is if you
> were afraid to go home to tell Lisa
> you're all moving to San Francisco.

Aaron is quiet for a moment, drinking. He turns to Jack.

> AARON
> This is a big thing.

> JACK
> Yeah.

> AARON
> Moving and... this is a big thing.

> JACK
> Yeah.

> AARON
> We're going to be okay?

> JACK
> I'll make sure that we are, Aaron.
> I promise.

Aaron looks at him for a moment.

> AARON
> Okay, Mr. CEO. I hope you're right
> about this.

> JACK
> Aren't I always, though?

LEAP YEAR, S2, EP. 1 "A TRAIN WRECK"   25.

They smile, clink glasses, and finish their drinks.

30   <u>EXT. C3D OFFICE – OUTSIDE – NIGHT</u>   30

The ALARM screams outside the office of C3D.

                                                    FADE TO BLACK.

Index

179